9780413 297808

METHUEN PLAYSCRIPTS

The Methuen Playscripts series exists to
extend the range of plays in print by publishing
work which is not yet widely known but
which has already earned a place in the
repertoire of the modern theatre.

The Fun Art Bus:
An Inter-Action Project by Ed Berman
Compiled by Justin Wintle

In 1972, its first year, the Fun Art Bus
(a converted double decker) toured the
London boroughs and other parts of
Britain presenting a unique combination
of entertainment and theatre for children
and adults. This volume contains an
account of the ideas of 'environmental
theatre' which are central to the work of
Inter-Action and of the Fun Art Bus
project. It also contains a selection of the
material performed on the Bus, including
short plays written for the Bus by Jim
Hiley, James Saunders, Chris Bailey,
Michael Stevens, Henry Livings, Frank
Marcus, David Halliwell and Neil Hornick.
It will be a valuable source book for
anyone concerned with youth and
community drama.

FUN ART BUS

An Inter-Action
Project
by Ed Berman

Compiled by
Justin Wintle

Published by
Eyre Methuen

First published in Great Britain 1973
by Eyre Methuen Ltd
11 New Fetter Lane London EC4P 4EE

Set by Expression Typesetters
Printed in Great Britain by
Redwood Press Limited, Trowbridge, Wiltshire

SBN 413 29780 2 Hardback
    413 29790 X Paperback

Compiler's Foreword

The Fun Art Bus is indebted to the generosity of all its artistic contributors, who made donations of their work. I would like to thank them and everyone at Inter-Action who either worked or performed on the project for giving me their time to discuss the Bus. In particular I would like to thank Noel Grieg, Jim Hiley and Neil Hornick for long, informative and enjoyable conversations, as well as Annette Drago and Heather Symons in the office for finding every file I mislaid, and many more besides. The death of Naftali Yavin deprived me of a key informant, though his ideas were so solid that they have not been hard to lay hands on. Finally my greatest thanks to Ed Berman, the creator and director of the Fun Art Bus, who provided me with the materials and helped organize them.

Justin Wintle

Contents

1: ENTER-INTER-TRANSPORT   7

2: MAKING A BUS   17

    — The Pedestrians' Bus   25
    — The Passengers' Bus   29

3: THE THEATRE ON THE UPPER DECK   33

    — from the Bus Repertoire:
    Jim Hiley   **How To Travel in Fun
                                               and Comfort**   34
    James Saunders   **Act**   35
    Chris Bailey   **Strong Right Arm Stuff**   37
    Michael Stevens   **We're All Going To
                                               Southampton**   42
    Frank Marcus   **Bus Trip**   45
    Henry Livings   **Shurrup**   49
    David Halliwell   **An Amour**   50
    — The Dogg's Troupe
    Leon Rosselson   **There's No Bussiness
                                               Like Show Bussiness**   58
    — The Other Company
    Neil Hornick   **The Bus Hijack Mystery**   67
    — The Thespian Show

4: THE FIRST SEASON OF THE FUN ART BUS   80

    AFTERWORD by Ed Berman   83

    APPENDIX Music to Leon Rosselson's Songs   85

Photographs by Rod Morrison

1: ENTER-INTER-TRANSPORT *

Lullaby to a Baby Bus

How far can a bus go,
How near is your stop,
Wherever you trip
Your bottom's your top.

Ascend to the stair
Ascend to the sky
Ascend to the ground
You're too low to fly.

The ground is on foot
The air on the wing
The wheel's on the round
You'll tire your spring.

Drive on drive out
Drive in drive round
You'll never drive up
Without running down.

(Prof. R. L. Dogg)

A theatre, a cinema, a planetarium – they are all buildings, but there is little about them to remind you of other buildings. The FUN ART BUS however is like any other double-decker – at least at first sight: it travels down the high street in the snarl of other traffic, it draws up at the lights, it stops to pick up passengers – ordinary passengers who, if they had been unlucky, might have boarded another bus. It is even red.

Look again. One side, the street side, has not two but five decks; the destination roller at the front is a fruit machine, spinning eyes, teeth and breasts as well as apples, bananas and oranges; at the back the other destination roller unwinds as a numerical proverb: '2-8-1' and an apple, which is reduced by stages to a core, thus – 'two ate one apple'. From the top window in the front of the Bus a crowd stares down at you; a Ralph Steadman cartoon issues instructions to motorists from the rear bottom window; and in the window above this, a clearly visible chunk of sky. If the Bus is at a standstill, it is likely you will find the driver playing an electric piano mounted on the bonnet beside him. A Bus conductor – possibly several conductors, all in special uniform – accompanies him with a guitar and words:

Come and take a ride on the Fun Art Bus
Come and take a ride down the street with us
Leave all your cares and your blues outside
Come along with us for a nice long ride
Don't be shy or slow, 'cos we're ready to go – on the Bus,
    On the Bus, on the Fun Art Bus.

*EIT is the formal name of the Fun Art Bus company. Parodying 'London Transport', EIT is one of the elaborate puns Ed Berman concocted to decorate the bus.

Come inside and seek what you want to find
Grab yourself a seat and relax your mind
Lots of things to do, lots of things to see
Needn't spend a p, you can travel free
You don't have to pay and we'll take you all the way — on the Bus,
    On the Bus, on the Fun Art Bus.

We've got a movie show in the downstairs part
Got some funny pictures and kinetic art
Just settle down and-a you will find
You're disappearing up the armpits of your mind
Got a long way to go, travel with the show — on the Bus,
    On the Bus, on the Fun Art Bus.

See the human puppets in the side window
Hear the driver thumping up on the pi-a-no
See the ol' conductor with his harp round his neck
Or watch them playing Hamlet on the topmost deck
Step right through the door you can leave your mother-in-law — on the Bus,
    On the Bus, on the FUN ART BUS.

    (Random 12 Bar — Trevor Crozier)

Look up from the pavement to the top deck: strange heads stare ahead or, turned sideways, gaze down at you: some of their faces have been cut out, and now the people you just saw climb on board are peering out through the spaces. Between the decks, in place of the usual strip advertisement for Guinness or a choice airline, you are told: FUN ART BUS; and between these big letters speech balloons conduct the dialogue of invisible conversants — 'What's it advertising?' — 'What's it in aid of?' — 'Just Fun!' — 'Are they students?' — 'Is it for kids?' — 'Taxi!' — 'Must be the Council doing us good again' — 'Is it a museum?' — 'No, it's free' — 'They call anything art these days' — 'It's free — it would have to be' — 'Do they make you do anything?' — 'You don't even have to laugh' — 'Bus — is it art?' — 'It's Inter-Action's Fun Art Bus'. If you stand well back, these speech balloons appear to be making a cartoon strip out of the living persons standing on the street giving their thoughts above their heads as the Bus draws up beside them.

In the side windows of the lower deck two people, real people (human puppets), face you through the glass, smiling, grimacing, gesturing at each other, reading a newspaper, or trying to push one another out of sight.

When you have watched them long enough, take heed of the instruction beneath, painted in the familiar gold lettering of London Transport: ENTER-INTER-TRANSPORT. Climb on board.

To your immediate left on the platform catch sight of the cinema screen at the end of the short side-bench section of the lower deck — 'The Smallest Cinema on Wheels'. Films or slide shows are running. Observe the 'Table of Fare': from Trafalgar Square it's 10p to Chalk Farm, £253.85 to Peking, £528.75 to Sydney, or £11,945.00 to the Sea of Tranquillity — figures all calculated from regulation London Transport distance charges. It's cheaper by plane if you want to go down under, but for the really long haul NASA can't compete. And then, before you put a foot on the stairs, take note of the country cottage tucked into

TABLE OF FARE

	TRAFALGAR SQUARE	SYDNEY	PEKING	NEW YORK	SEA OF TRANQUILITY (MOON)	HONG KONG	CHALK FARM	CALCUTTA	BAHAMAS (NASSAU)
ATHENS	£75.05	£476.10	£236.85	£246.05	£11945.00	£265.50	£75.05	£196.25	£286.85
BAHAMAS (NASSAU)	£216.75	£473.85	£393.40	£54.80	£11945.00	£453.55	£216.75	£451.85	
CALCUTTA	£248.10	£283.95	£100.90	£395.90	£11945.00	£82.10	£248.10		
CHALK FARM	£00.10	£528.75	£253.85	£172.00	£11945.00	£299.65			
HONG KONG	£299.65	£229.25	£60.65	£402.75	£11945.00				
SEA OF TRANQUILITY (MOON)	£11945.00	£11945.00	£11945.00	£11945.00					
NEW YORK	£172.00	£497.45	£342.10						
PEKING	£253.85	£277.90							
SYDNEY	£528.75								

PLEASE KEEP YOUR TICKET   YOU MAY WANT TO SHOW IT

PLEASE KEEP YOUR COOL   YOU MAY WANT TO SHOW IT

PLEASE KEEP YOUR MONEY   YOU MAY WANT TO SHOW IT

Dog's are allowed on board at conductor's discretion. Dogs must pay the same fare as children. Children must pay the same fare as adults. Fair's Fare. Neither dogs, nor children, nor adults, regardless of their fare, may foul the floor or score goals on the upper deck.

* This table is derived by the simple formula of multiplying the number of miles (point-to-point) by the regulated London Transport fare charge. Thus, for example, the commercial price by jet to Sydney from London is £195; the London Transport price by diesel engine would be £528.75. London Transport does not run a route to Sydney, however. In any case, it could only charge a maximum of 20p.

the luggage compartment, of the camera mounted on the white wood panelling above it, of the antlers, of the crazy paving laid out on the alighting platform. The staircase itself you will recognize — it is of the traditional cosy cottage flying ducks variety, replete with flowered wallpaper and a bright white bannister. Go up — you will soon have your head among the clouds, literally; you have been brought eye-level with a sunset.

It's darker on the top deck. Except what little light comes in through the cut-outs on the left hand side, four small spotlights, trained on a plush red curtain up at the front end, provide the only other illumination. The curtain is set in a proscenium arch: this parody of a bus parodies traditional theatre well as. As your eyes adjust you notice the ordinary bus seats. But on the floor there is grass, and the walls and the ceiling of the deck change colours like a rainbow. Find somewhere to sit. If you haven't had one already, a conductor gives you a ticket. It's free, so don't put your hand in your pocket. Read it. Perhaps it is Roger Mcgough's 'Poem for President Nixon' — ' . . . let saigons . . . be saigons . . . '. Tickets are transferable: pass yours to your neighbour, and receive another in return:

And there are plenty more if you want to swap with someone across the aisle.

LULLABY TO A BABY BUS
How far can a bus go
How near is your stop
Wherever you trip
Your bottom's your top.
Ascend to the stair
Ascend to the sky
Ascend to the ground
You're too low to fly.
The ground is on foot
The air on the wing
The wheels on the round
You'll tire your spring.
Drive on drive out
Drive in drive round
You'll never drive up
Without running down.
Prof. R. L. Dogg
Fun Art Bus
Transferable

VICTORIAN Conversation Still Being Overheard OMNIBUS
God A fraud?!! My word Absurd.
Man A plan?!! In deed which creed.
Anon.
Fun Art Bus
Transferable

Old & Directionless

The old bus conductor

Driving the old bus

Along the same old route

Thinks

The same old thoughts

Brian Patten

Fun Art Bus

Transferable

EARLY MORN'NG

POEM No. 1

Got up
did my toilet
washed
shaved
combed hair

(my toilet
looks much
nicer now)

Roger Mc gough

EARLY MORNING

POEM No. 2

Got up
had shave
did Times crossword
had another shave

Roger Mc gough

Fun Art Bus

Transferable

---

ticket

i have at last
become lazy
too slow and tired
to climb the stairs,
sit in the long seat
think of cigarettes
and look out to the
horizons set me
by the edges
of this ticket.

Peter Finch

Fun Art Bus

Transferable

buzzbus

(to be whispered
to the person
next to you)

bus
buzz buzz
broozz buzz
brown blue bus
booze buzz
blues bus
boos buzz
boos bust
whose bus?

Peter Finch

Fun Art Bus

Transferable

---

4 p.m. spring

kids spilling out
onto the angel
dust seeds rise
in carpets
down the goswell rd,

their pail disc faces.

Hugh Lauder

Fun Art Bus

Transferable

Ticket Poem

I wanted one life
you wanted another
we couldn't have
one cake
so we ate each other

Roger Mc gough

Fun Art Bus

Transferable

ACROSTICKETS

I

Frantically
Unfunny
Nonsense

Arrives
Rather
Tardily

Behind
Usual
Schedule

I I

Family
Underwear
Needs

Adjusting
Round
The

B
U
S
t

Anon

Fun Art Bus

Transferable

POEM FOR NATIONAL L.S.D.* WEEK	Untitled & Unnumbered Bus Poem 2	Poem For President Nixon
Mind How you Go !!!	If you get a Buzz from this Bus There's probably A Bee in its Bonnet	. . . let saigons . . . . be saigons . . .
* or pot, cannabis or whatever	You may Believe Plastic grass is the cause But it can't be with Plastic fuzz on it.	Roger Mc gough
Roger Mc gough		
Fun Art Bus	Fun Art Bus	Fun Art Bus
Transferable	Transferable	Transferable

The Bus lurches forward. A head appears through the curtain which has started to rustle; or a passenger you had been paying no particular attention to in the seat behind starts gasping because she thinks her baby's coming. Anything is about to happen. A show begins.

Thirty minutes or an hour later the Bus stops. You climb down the stairs and find yourself exactly where you were when it all began. Before alighting, put your ticket in the 'Used Poetry' container, and throw a backward glance at that camera, because the conductor is giving you a souvenir photograph: if you're expecting a photograph of yourself, do not be disappointed – you are holding Ed Berman's Self-Illustrating Post Card, showing a universal ghost figure stepping onto the Fun Art Bus from behind: the flash which struck your eyes as you stepped onto the Bus at the beginning has resulted in this protracted visual pun. Now draw your own image in the blank figure space.

You are also handed a cut-out model sheet of the Bus, and your own copy of Alan Brownjohn's 'Little Red Bus Book', with its blue cover, which tells you what to do on other routes. Suggestions include that you should:

START TODAY ON THE NO. 1 BUS.
WHERE IT CROSSES THE ROUTE OF
THE NO. 2, JOIN THE NO. 2 – AND
SO ON WITH NOS. 3, 4, 5 etc. LATE
AT NIGHT, LEAVE THE LAST 84 AND
JUMP ON A NIGHT-SERVICE N85
(CHARING CROSS EMBANKMENT).
CARRY ON NEXT DAY. AND EVERY
DAY.

choose your favourite bus, say a 36, and issue invitations to a Journey Reunion for Passengers to be held somewhere on the route two weeks later. At the Reunion, hold a debate on everyone's journeys and reasons for them, and if they're happy with reasons and journeys, and if not why not. Compose songs or a small opera on the travels and travails of the 36. End with food and drink

board a bus travelling through Notting Hill. Politely ask anyone *not* getting off, 'It's obviously fun to live here, isn't it?' If they answer emphatically Yes, pass on. If they answer emphatically No, pass on saying, 'Thank you'. If they answer either way uncertainly, hold a politico-philosophical discussion on 'Fun and Notting Hill'

on a fast bus on a hilly journey (e.g. Denmark Hill to Dulwich) swing hand by hand from handrail to handrail upstairs singing, 'You don't need trees to be Tarzan'.

begin at the beginning of a route, upstairs in the back seat. Watch to see which of the first twelve people boarding after you gets off last. Award him a specially designed Long Journey Certificate

board a bus travelling through South Kensington. Politely ask anyone *not* getting off, 'It's obviously fun to live here, isn't it?' If they answer emphatically Yes, pass on. If they answer emphatically No, or answer either way uncertainly, hold a philosophico-political discussion on 'Fun and South Kensington'

give out ball-point pens on a bus and award a Plain-Clothes Fun Bus Doughnut (e.g. a stick of celery or a sardine on toast) for the best cartoon/poem/ statement of a philosophy of

3/4. *Self Illustrating Post Card*

Fun Art Bus of Inter-Action
This completely redesigned red double decker bus was originally created for the Festivals of London 1972 and granted approval by London Transport to run 16 routes in London. The bus is staffed by either the Dogg's Troupe or the Bus Company.

Devised: Ed Berman   Photograph: Rod Morrison   Printer: Hill & Garwood Printing Wembley England

Self-Illustrating Postcard
Carte Postale Commemorative Individualisee
Selbst Illustrierte Post Karte

life done in ten minutes on the
back of a ticket.

give out a sheet of paper and a pencil to
travellers on a bus in any area. The
idea is, work out how long it would take
travelling day and night, week by week,
month by month, to spend as much on
bus fares as you would need to buy a
£50,000 house in Chelsea. On the other
side of the sheet it asks: if it takes a
short time, what might be wrong with
the fares? If it takes a long time would
it be more economic living with sand-
wiches, thermos, sleeping bag and
Complete Shakespeare on a comfortable
London bus?

on the one hot, blistering day this
summer, follow a tired white man
onto a bus where the others are
coloured. Ask him if he knows where
in the world a white man would feel
legally bound, or happy or dignified
sweating in the sun till the next bus
came. (A black man on a white bus
might know.)

Hire a bus and have a one-day
travelling Republic. Serve Republican
food and drink

And as you finally get off, the buskers are already on the pavement singing
another song to prospective passengers:

CHORUS: The Fun Art Bus is the bus of the people*
              Step on board the Fun Art Bus,
              No need to rush,
              Don't have to fuss,
              If you come with us
              On the Fun Art Bus,
              Step on board the bus of the people
              Step on board the Fun Art Bus.

Of all the inventions the world has ever seen,
Like the telephone, the motor car and margarine,

*Originally, 'The Fun Art Bus is the Bus of the Future'. When Leon delivered the song,
everybody was delighted. Ed Berman was also puzzled: 'We're about people in the
streets, not a technological mystery tour.' So it became 'The Bus of the People'.

5. THE FUN ART BUS

There's none can compare with this magical machine,
This magical machine, the Fun Art Bus.

CHORUS

Come on all you ladies and take a trip today,
You can travel any distance and you won't have to pay,
You can get off where you like, you can go all the way,
You can go all the way on the Fun Art Bus.

CHORUS

You can have your photo taken, you can wear a funny hat,
You can sing, you can joke, you can have a little chat,
You can do what you fancy if you fancy that,
If you fancy that on the Fun Art Bus.

CHORUS

So come on all you people and take a little ride,
Never mind if you're twenty stone and five foot wide,
There'll be room for you, just roll inside,
Just roll inside the Fun Art Bus.

CHORUS

If buses were fun and buses were free,
We wouldn't have to travel in misery,
And a bus ride would be like a holiday spree,
A holiday spree on the Fun Art Bus.

CHORUS

(Bus of the People — Leon Rosselson)

And it must not be supposed that those cooped up all day in a fourth floor
office miss out on all the fun: they have only to look out of their windows, and
they might just see a whole garden bustling down the street, planted, somehow,
on the roof of a red double decker. The idea? Something for everyone, from
every angle.

2: Making a Bus

The Fun Art Bus is run by Inter-Action. The following letter, written when the Bus was still at a planning stage, outlines how such a project fits into the complex network of community and arts activities which comprise the organization:

January 1972

Dear Justin,

I think it might be useful to write a book about the Fun Art Bus. Since our discussion it has become clear that I have no time to write. Will you 'edit'/write an account of the bus?

If you accept this proposal I would want to monitor the book closely. It should show the Bus in the context of Inter-Action.

The Trust is built on the premise of trying to relate the arts (and artists) to the needs of living communities. These may be isolated groups who are institutionalized (such as mental hospitals, remand homes, old age homes, schools, etc.), common interest groups (like experimental theatre buffs, claimants unions, working people in a neighbourhood who share a similar lunchtime), or simply people living in the same area.

It seems to me that creative people who care (call them artists if you must) can make important contributions in these areas. They can explore, experiment and initiate outside of worn-out traditions and repressive structures.

The problems of a pluralist urban society (and an over-populated one dependent on machines as well) are very complex. Answers, if there are any, lie in the ability to relate, to inform, to listen — in short the abilities of creative people. It is unfortunate that they have to be categorized as artists and even more sad that their work must be product-orientated and sold as a commodity in order for its importance to emerge.

In our twelve divisions of work we emphasize the motivating element of fun. Thus, I have great hopes that the Fun Art Bus will form another possibility to bring people together. The essence of this positive (non-tragic) side of our lives seems to move from Fun to Enjoyment to Joy to Love. It is essentially this 'comic' side we are dealing with and I suppose different people use different words from the spectrum to spell out that positive coming together/community/communion.

Obviously the Bus will bring many elements of our work together as well as people — music, poetry, plays, films, design, painting, and basic craft skills. Of ultimate importance is the fact that it will go to where people are and will treat with them on home ground. It will not be an elitist palace where only the informed and the fortunate can go for their special treatment.

Naturally we will use it a great deal in our home territory, Kentish Town West, Camden. But from here it will go out in a sort of rippling pattern, emphasizing our responsibility to neighbouring communities in North London, and correspondingly less to inhabitants of Skegness or the Outer Hebrides.

Sincerely,

Ed Berman

P.S. A Bus trip will never be the same for a Hampstead mater, a Cockney pater or a child starved of magic in the conveyor belt called 'education' and cossetted by the seat belt called Theatre-In-Education.

The Bus grew out of the plans of an earlier Inter-Action project, the Mobile Base, masterminded by Ed in 1970. This idea was, in retrospect, premature, and for financial reasons never got off the ground. Needless to say mobility was to have been the Base's chief recommendation. Similar in size to a bus, one entire side was to have lowered out, like a drawbridge, to form a rostrum-stage for Inter-Action's professional theatre groups, or a launching deck for participatory street plays. Films would have been projected onto the rear of the transport, provision was made for a peep-hole theatre, and sound and video equipment would have been at the disposal of staff and audiences. With ten or so members of Inter-Action tied to the Base, there would have been a generous selection of the Trust's skills: creative work with young people, training courses for group and community work — with particular facilities for areas of extreme social and cultural deprivation — and, on a mixed media basis, the theatrical activities. Inter-Action receives constant requests to take its work to localities on both sides of the Atlantic. The Base was one solution to the problems involved in meeting these demands.

Entertainment, as 'an opening wedge into closed communities', was fundamental to these plans. It will be seen that much of the thinking behind the Mobile Base, in this and in other respects, was carried through into the Fun Art Bus, and often embellished, even if the temptation to put quite so many goodies in one basket had to be resisted.

THE FUN ART BUS

Ed revived and revised his ideas in the Spring of 1971. It became clear that the conversion of an ordinary London Transport double-decker would be cheaper to run and just as exciting as the Base. It would also give him the opportunity to put environmental theatre on a new footing, by providing people with a ready-made environment they could relate to out of their normal experience. By June, he was ready to announce to the Press that London Transport and the Greater London Arts Association had given Inter-Action the go-ahead to run the project in the Festivals of London 1972. A bus was purchased in December, and in January the real work began.

The first task was to organize the creation of materials. Ed wanted to challenge the artistic community of Great Britain, to see what it could offer for his popular arts venture, and gauge how it reacted to his proposals. A circular letter was sent out to hundreds of artists, composers, cartoonists, poets and dramatists, inviting them to make a contribution. Enclosed with the letter were three closely typed pages of briefing notes stating the kind of material he wanted, and the equipment that would be available. These notes began with the General Purpose:

> The idea is to create an artistic entity which will travel the streets of London making the art of fun freely available to anyone who wishes to climb aboard . . .

We wish to create an integrated whole, retaining the character, even the colour, of a London Transport Bus; but to have music, drama, films, words, sounds, space and visuals, creating a meaningful experience for the passengers on a unique trip.

Following a section in which objects and events that might confront passengers on a possible journey were described, the second page checked out the hardware and other facilities: a closed circuit television system, the proscenium stage upstairs, the availability of a cast of at least four actors and actresses, an elaborate sound speaker system, the electric piano on the bonnet, the additional musical skills of the conductors, as well as all the external and internal surfaces and spaces of the Bus which required artwork. And finally, on the last page, Ed's 'Notes for Composers, Writers, Choreographers and Visual Artists':

There are three types of programme categories to be slotted in the bus you may wish to create for:

1. Family Entertainment
2. Children
3. X Certificate

I think these are self-explanatory. Use your own judgement; I shall have to use mine. You may wish to create something for all three or just one.

Audience Situation: There will be times when children only will come on the bus (picking up kids from school). There will be occasions when the bus will function as the most avant-garde of theatres and warnings will be posted that the route is dangerous for children and other immature minds. There will be the random situation as well, when anyone of any age might get on at a stop.

****

More important than the above is the thematic line of the categories. I am setting no limits, but −

1. I would prefer something written for the actual environment, i.e. a bus passing through time and space as it does normally.
2. On the other hand, anything on any subject you would like that would fit into the media we are using would be acceptable (bearing in mind the size restrictions).

We will have a CCTV system (½" tape) so that the limitation is one of writing for a small studio situation. There will be the tiny 'proscenium stage' upstairs with a cast of four (two males, two females, mixed racially), but you can use the driver as an off-stage voice and the clippie and a number of 'actors' in the seats.

Sounds composed for the speaker system have virtually no limitations unless you want the RPO and they happen to be busy on recording day.

Ballet will be more difficult. Opera is obviously simple.

Remember there is noise on a moving bus. (We will have at least one superb mime in the company.) And there will be life in the audience, the comings and goings of passengers.

Time limits are perhaps from several seconds to fifteen minutes. But a running line throughout the trip would also be fine. I hope to have 3 one-hour shows for live theatre and for CCTV working alternately upstairs, and at least 3 changes of visuals and sounds.

This is not meant to be a gimmick nor a vehicle for topical revue. It is meant to be a creation on its own — The Fun Art Bus.

Ed hoped that there would be enough artists with that slightly quirky imaginative quality necessary for the project. He never pretended that it was something everybody had the ability to create for. But, for anybody prepared to write or design to order and not simply out of the top of his head there was certainly plenty of scope. People who had good ideas and wanted to know more were offered the closest co-operative working conditions, in so far as these would improve the product, during the last two months of preparations and rehearsals. The demands, although precise, did not seem over-strenuous. There was of course no money, but then as it would have been quite unfeasible to pay all the contributors without charging the passengers for the ride, this did not seem unreasonable: many of the artists who were canvassed were established commercially anyway.

As expected, the response to the letter and briefing notes was varied, though on occasion unexpectedly venomous. Less than a quarter of the material performed or worked into the Bus resulted from this blanket appeal; most of what came in this way wasn't used. Some writers scribbled an idea down on a scrap of paper and contented themselves they had fulfilled a duty. Some were highly exceptious that there was no money involved. Others opened their dusty drawers and sent in whatever they pulled out. Many rose excitedly to the idea, but failed to lift their muses with them, apologizing that their typewriters had spavins, or even that they were simply too tired at the moment. One or two leapt to an attack that was more bristled than bristling. Olwen Wymark, for example, wrote:

Dear Ed,

Thank you for your letter about the FUn ArT bUs.

I'm sorry to say that rather than being 'enticed' I am really more repelled. It feels to me like patronage bordering on contempt — for the passengers (audience) and it also sounds like a new and very refined kind of torture and finally it typifies for me the trend that I feel is going on nowadays — e.g. 'we know what art is *and* what fun is and you're going to get it whether you like it or not.'

I felt this very strongly about the Flea Circus too.

Sorry but truthfully,

Olwen Wymark

N.B. It also seems to like me a *terrible* waste of money.

Ed replied, giving her more perhaps than she deserved:

Dear Olwen,

Having received your reply to my request for artistic contributions to the Fun Art Bus over a month ago, I have remained silent, I suppose, in the face of an enemy. I certainly hope that there is no animosity towards our work on your part, but I can find no other reason for your writing such a letter.

You say that the idea of the bus repels you, seeming to be more like patronage bordering on contempt for the passengers resembling a new and very refined kind of torture, ultimately cramming one person's artistic opinions down the throats of others.

There is something faintly absurd about this logic, but I shall attempt to deal with it as best I can. I do not believe that art has to be serious or bitter in order for it to be effective. Why comic art should be any more contemptuous of its audience than any other form is quite beyond me.

I find that the old-fashioned forms of theatre are exquisitely refined forms of torture which prevent most people from coming and going as they please, or making comments during the period of sacred ritual. It seems to me that a Bus, which allows for easy access and rejection is hardly cramming anything down somebody's throat, would be limited torture if it were torture at all, and has very much a kind of motorized troubador approach, which far from being contemptuous seems to adapt a tradition to a modern age.

As for people claiming they know what art is, I should think that playwrights who script things for delivery by puppets calling themselves actors and directors, are far more worthy of your criticism than we are. Any artist who functions regardless of his modesty is in fact saying he knows what his art is or he would not practise it presumably.

As for it being a terrible waste of money, it will cost less than a fifth of the cost of mounting a West End production, be available to people regardless of their backgrounds or geographical location in relation to the palaces of culture, and will be seen and participated in by thousands of people, without enormous expenditure.

While I regret that we do not agree on the community and communication roles of theatre I find that your objections to our projects except where they are in the most formal or elite of settings, are purely emotional ones. I suppose I would applaud this difference of opinion if I were liberal, but since it smacks of the elitism which I abhor in the arts world, I can only hope for the waxing of our approach and the waning of yours.

With regrets and sincerely,

Ed Berman

Olwen Wymark was not alone in her belief that comic art is necessarily more condescending toward its audience than other forms. Arnold Wesker at least paid Ed the compliment of choosing his words:

Dear Ed,

It's no use pretending, but the very notion of a Fun Art Bus sends cold shivers right through me. It carries overtones of 'Is everybody happy?'. And forced gaiety is guaranteed to produce gloom. Anyway, although I would love to be out there in the democratic ranks I just don't think I can earn my place there by kidding them art is funny.

I think you are a very energetic and engaging personality but ever since I heard you propound the notion that individual artists are fascists, I just don't think we would ever be talking about the same things.

May God bless you in your endeavours to make it a funny world.
Yours,

Arnold Wesker

and was paid for his pains with this reply:

Dear Arnold,

I regret to say there is no God and it is a funny world, regardless of my endeavours or those ascribed to him.

I regret that the Fun Art Bus idea sends cold shivers through you. I have always found it interesting that whenever we have discussed people and art you have used an 'us and them' vocabulary, such as 'I would love to be out there in the democratic ranks'. It is characteristic of elite artists to write from ivory towers about things they have no actual need to be identified with.

Understandably enough you take art very seriously because for you it is a matter of money and pretence. There is no question in my mind that art is either funny or unfunny. Some art or artifice can be funny and some can be serious, but I do not particularly see tragedy as being higher than comedy on an imaginary scale of elitist values.

By the way, you can't kid somebody that something is funny. It either is or is not funny. I have never propounded the idea that individual artists are fascists, not at least in such an extreme way as you would have it. But I believe it is a fair polarization of our views. Just to get the record straight, my view is that to say one thing and do another is lying. Lying to people on a mass scale is a totalitarian approach to society. When an artist sets himself up to speak to large numbers of people about something he claims to have first-hand knowledge of but in fact is only guessing at, and where he does not share the predicament of the people he is talking to or writing about and has only an intellectual appreciation of this predicament, then I feel he is lying; and he is lying for the purpose of ego or money, which I consider to be a further complication in the case.

If an artist further sets up what is meant to be a dialogue and then refuses to let one part of the equation speak, he is being repressive.

All this does not mean that I believe the only kind of play is one in which the audience can participate, nor does it mean, as you can see, that all individual artists are fascists. It simply means what it says, and if the shoe fits I dare say people will feel uncomfortable in the face of it, because they say one thing and do another. Which all leaves me a bit puzzled as to why you can take such fright whenever there is an attempt to create a dialogue between us.

I take it that you understand that my remarks are not in any way personally or maliciously intended. I simply do not understand your position, which seems to me untenable, and I should like to create an occasion or means by which we can discuss it, but if either of us feels that the other is totally wrong then that is perhaps just reason for you to write to me in the way you do.

All the best,
Ed Berman

Others were less willing to be side-tracked into the differences between Fun and Funniness or comedy. John Osborne confessed: 'I am afraid I am really quite certain I have nothing to contribute to this sort of enterprise'. Harold Pinter's characteristic pithiness insisted on giving nothing away: 'I'm afraid I can't' he wrote.

The positive responses however, from both established and unestablished artists, were sufficient, as the Bus was to demonstrate.

As the replies and materials thickened toward April 1st, the date provisionally fixed for the start of rehearsals, the Bus itself was prepared. It had been agreed in the autumn of 1971 that the Art College of Ealing Polytechnic would handle the basic reconstruction of the interior. Ideas for the re-orientation of the physical plans proliferated at a meeting held between Ed and the staff and students of the college early in January. Originally intended for the lower deck, the theatre was now shifted upstairs to be combined with the CCTV, to give writers the opportunity to use both media simultaneously. The lower deck was to be partitioned off into a cinema, occupying the side-bench section just inside the entrance, and, behind this, the dressing-cum-controls-cum-projection room with space for the window-box theatre.

Ed's basic guideline was that the vehicle should be kept 'looking like a bus, only bizarre and fun'. He also made elaborately detailed practical demands and suggestions to force the craftsmen to produce an integrated experience. Replacements must be found for the interior advertising spaces. Could the passenger's bell be fixed so that it played a tune when pressed? What would be the best visual art construction for the luggage compartment under the stairs. What about inflatable seat covers? He insisted that there should be not one, but two trap-doors up through the ceiling of the controls room into the stage area which was created by removing the front two seats on either side of the top deck. It was necessary too that there should be adequate ventilation to prevent the passengers from stewing beneath the four spotlights which were to be placed above them in front of the proscenium arch: all the windows were being covered over with wood and aluminium to keep the light out of the theatre and provide more space for artwork externally, so there was no natural draught; eventually small air-flues were let in to the roof of the Bus. The proscenium arch itself had to be fixed so that, while retaining the look of a proscenium arch, it didn't get in the way of the audience, the actors and the television system; and the televison had to be fixed so that it didn't get in the way of the actors when it wasn't in use, which meant constructing an arm-platform that swung in and out of the side of the acting area behind the arch. The acting area was no more than a six-foot cube, so these operations had to be carried out with the utmost economy of space. All this had to be done before the surfaces inside the upper deck were decorated. The walls and the ceiling needed something special, but also something that wouldn't interfere with the theatrical activities. And should something be done to the floor?

Power presented an almost insuperable difficulty. It was out of the question that the sound, lighting and visual systems could be run off the Bus's own engine. Obviously there had to be a special generator — but everybody was frightened by the noise it would make, let alone by its potential size. Playing for safety it was decided that a 4 kwt machine would have to do. This meant that although all the systems could be fed, they must not be fed simultaneously, even though, at a later stage, this threatened to increase the delicacy of programming a Bus trip several hundred per cent. To have had a larger generator – 6 kwt would have been ideal – would have meant towing a trailer behind the Bus, and this would have destroyed the illusion that it was like any other bus. It turned out well: the generator chosen was housed in a thoroughly sound-proofed wooden case in the controls room directly beneath the stage, providing the actors with a useful table as well.

There were problems of greater detail, but not of readier solubility. For instance, printing the Bus Tickets, so that the poems came out of the ticket machine in the right lengths. The production manager had been told by a printer that it would be easy to have them printed economically on the original paper rolls, but this proved incorrect. It was not until a week before the Bus was due on the road that the National Cash Register Company came to the rescue where every other company had failed.

Then there was the whole exterior. During March the designers argued with Ed about what could be done to the off or road side of the Bus. It had to be something startling, arresting. Inter-Action's own designer, Emmanuel Sandreuter, suggested an enormous replica of a television set; Shirtsleeves thought a plain brick wall best, possibly with a picture of an inverted bus hanging in the middle. Both these ideas were attractive, but neither quite fitted the bill – they were, if anything, too dramatic: Ed wanted something closer to reality. A week before the final decision had to be taken, he came up with the five-deck idea, which was then quickly designed by Emmanuel with an appropriate complement of identical passengers at each level. Ed then led a group poetry brainstorming session and came up with a series of satirical advertising slogans in three word units to be inserted between the five rows of windows:

MISS TAKE ME	FELT UNDER FELT	SLIP SHOD SHOE
REAP EAT REPEAT	DRINK PUNCH DRUNK	JOIN UP JOINT
EARN YEARN EARN	CRAVE SAVE SLAVE	SMOKE CHOKE CROAK
SPEND THRIFT LEND	INVEST GOES BUST	BYE BYE CYCLE

Since the initial season the five decks have been reduced to three: the impact is the same, but more credible.

Similarly, for some time nobody knew quite what to do with the front and back rollers – the destination indicators that are normally hand-turned. The opportunity to motorize them was taken, but the question of content still remained. Ed wanted poems or short stories that could be read easily from the pavement. The perfect texts were still to be written when Liz Leyh suggested a fruit machine instead for the front roller, and Ed continued the theme at the back with his apple pun, a childhood memory of a typical Yankee joke from his father. Every detail of the exterior was mulled over and charged with fun, right down to the wheel hubs, which now carry the legend EIT. The original company registration number of the Bus, RT 230, inscribed on each side of the driver's cab, was altered to RT? 0½ (Arty? Not half!). The planting of the roof garden coincided with the emergence of the cover-theme for the interior decoration: a juxtaposition of outdoor and indoor elements in the same space.

Rehearsals started in the second week of April: two companies – the Dogg's

Troupe and The Other Company — four one-hour shows, three directors — Ed, Noel Grieg and Naftali Yavin — and a first class stage management. In addition there were two hours of teletape to be filmed by Inter-Action's film and video units, using members of the same acting companies, and jam sessions for the recorded music. One hour's worth of the tele material was planned in a single day's brain-storming in a basement room in Islington amongst a group of writers, some of whom were already heavily committed to the Bus in other ways. The other hour was prepared by Paul Morrison, responsible for the Inter-Action subsidiary Infilms, after it had been scripted by Steve Jacobs. Ed asked Stephen Lewis and Bob Grant to join in with an experiment — video-taping an improvisation to be used as a final show. They came to the TV studio loaned by Stanley Hyland of Hi-Vision in Covent Garden, and improvised a special version of their popular television show 'On The Buses' — naturally this became 'On the Bus'.

The Bus was completed at Ealing a few hours before the first dress rehearsal on May 1st. Many features were not ready on time, and some had to be abandoned. there were supposed to have been two-dimensional survival packs and toilets as well as three-dimensional chains on the back of each seat upstairs in the theatre deck, headphones for every passenger, giant stand-up figures and an Inter-Action bus-stop to go out on the pavement, and a four-minute play from Tom Stoppard called *Hamlet* for two characters (' . . . one's Hamlet, the other isn't . . . '). But Ed wasn't worried: things were to be added and changed all the time; there must be no apparent finish to the creative process, else the product is dead. In any case he had planned the whole operation with a deli-berate policy of overkill, hedging his bets wherever he could to minimize the risk of being shortweighted.

Ed now concentrated all his energies toward helping the companies adapt from rehearsing in quiet rooms to performing in a moving bus: which isn't easy as it is often difficult just to stand still in such circumstances. And then at the last moment the whole project was almost confounded when it appeared that no firm was willing to undertake insurance of the passengers; Ed rang the Press, stories came out, and the insurance came through. On May 3rd, a day before the first official commitment in the London Boroughs, the Bus went on a trial run with a group of pensioners. From the reactions of these old people, totally without any inhibitions as regards this novel form of entertainment, it was immediately apparent that the Fun Art Bus was going to score in a big way; as a popular arts experiment it was going to be popular regardless of age or the social background of the audience.

THE PEDESTRIANS' BUS

Inter-Action has had a long involvement with both Street and Environmental theatre, dating back to its origins in 1968, when Ed first operated a window-cut-in that opened straight out onto a pavement in Notting Hill, human puppets performing for the benefit of passers-by. Wherever possible this pattern has been adopted in subsequent Inter-Action projects — the current Almost Free Theatre in Rupert Street, for example, has similar windows that allow for a maximum exposure, and the Bus has its own Kinetic Window Box Theatre, to attract people inside by holding their attention first. It is a practice based on a clearly conceived analysis of the mechanics of street theatre, beginning with the premise that the two basic elements — audience and players — are, in the first instance, mobile, and that, through the agency of sustained activity, either or both of these are available to be fixed. A procession of carnival floats is an example of a situation in which the audience is fixed, or arrested, on the pavement by a continuous succession of entertaining mobiles. Window shopping is a simple example of the complementary situation. Ed claims in fact that his earliest ventures in street theatre grew out of, amongst other things, an academic

6. *The Kinetic Window Box Theatre*

interest in the prostitutes' windows in Amsterdam, and in the herhane, or brothel compounds, found in Turkey, where he researched as a Rhodes Scholar. He does not shun the connotation of voyeuristic motivations, but is willing to play along with them. The Kinetic Window Boxes face out on the pavement side of the Fun Art Bus. The human puppets in these window-theatres establish eye contact with pedestrians who are by this time probably eyeing the bus in a state of wary disbelief. This state has undoubtedly been precipitated by their initial sighting of the Bus itself, the noise of the electric piano or of the Bus Signature Tune as it is played over the external speaker system, and by the antics of the Bus Company performing on the pavement in their unusual uniforms.

In the Kinetic Window Boxes of the Fun Art Bus the human puppets, instead of being seen in profile as passengers are usually seen in the windows of a bus, face the pedestrians directly. In normal circumstances there are two human puppets, doing things one might not notice if they were done elsewhere, and doing them with a tight clockwork rhythm.

Ed wanted the Kinetic Boxes to consist of two windows, side by side, one for the live figures and one for a set of cards, so that the human puppets would be seen to react to a series of images brought up in the window next to them, employing a visual fiction similar to that of headlines on newspapers in strip cartoons. But, given the limited amount of space in the controls room behind the windows, it proved impossible to devise a machinery that would turn enough cards fast enough for this to work, so in the end he had to rely completely on what the human puppets could do between themselves. Max Eisenberg, Peter Frankham, Annette Drago and Peter Southcott, the four members of Inter-Action who usually played in the windows in pairs, performed a number of sketches which Ed created and dictated into a cassette en route to the first performance. The performers later added other sketches under Peter Frankham's guidance. Each sketch is a routine of movements or gestures, sometimes based on one or two simple props. For example, in *Newspaper*, two human puppets dressed as a hippy and a businessman appear in the window reading 'Melody Maker' and the 'Financial Times' respectively, facing straight out onto the pavement: Thus:

1. The hippy and the businessman read their papers, holding them up so that their faces cannot be seen.
2. Simultaneously they lower their papers.
3. The hippy lifts his paper again and resumes reading.
4. The businessman lifts his paper.
5. The hippy lowers his paper.
6. The hippy leans over and starts reading the businessman's paper.
7. The businessman lowers his paper.
8. The businessman looks accusingly at the hippy.
9. Both the hippy and the businessman return to reading their own papers.

    (Double pause)

10. They both lower their papers.
11. The businessman lifts his paper again.
12. The hippy lifts his paper.
13. The businessman lowers his paper.

14. The businessman leans over and starts reading the hippy's paper.
15. The hippy lowers his paper.
16. The hippy looks accusingly at the businessman.
17. Both the businessman and the hippy return to reading their own papers.
18. They both lower their papers . . .
19. . . . and look at each other.
20. They smile at each other.
21. Then, very seriously, they look out front.
22. The hippy and the businessman lift up their papers.
23. They lower their papers and, simultaneously, bow to the audience.

The essence of this piece was the unfortunate isolation of two basically similar human beings, hiding behind their trappings and their reading matter.

Each action was given a five second interval: a metronomic rhythm pattern was vital if the sketches were to hold the attention of passers-by as well as capture it. This technique worked particularly well in another sketch, *See-saw*, in which the two human puppets, A and B, are dressed identically:

1. A comes up in the window and smiles enthusiastically at the pedestrians.
2. B comes up beside A with an expression of anger. B begins to push A down, his expression changing to one of happiness.
3. A goes down, disappearing, a very unhappy expression.
4. B remains, smiling.
5. A comes up again, and starts pushing B down. The appropriate changes in expression are repeated.
6. B goes down.
7. A remains, very happy.
8. Rather more quickly, B comes up and pushes A down.
9. A goes down.
10. B remains, very happy.
11. Even more quickly, A comes up and pushes B out of sight.
12. A remains, extremely happy.
13. B comes up very quickly and pushes A out of sight.
14. B smiles.
15. A's hand comes up and grabs B's throat to pull him down.
16. Strangled, B disappears.

Perhaps the point here is that there is not enough space in a tight little box for two people to be happy at one time.

There were many other sketches. For example, Peter Frankham worked up a couple of cigarette advertisements: in the first, a smoke bomb goes off behind a human puppet who is smoking — it is uncertain whether he is being choked by the cigarette or by the bomb; in the second another human puppet, unaware that his friend is trying to show the pedestrians how to smoke, comes up and begins cleaning the window, from the inside, blotting out the audience's view. At other times one or two human puppets sat in the window and, with or without props, reacted directly to the pedestrians looking in.

On the pavement itself there is more live entertainment to encourage people's interest. In the first season whichever company — Dogg's or TOC — was performing on the day would come down from the theatre to the street and join

Trevor and Annie Crozier, who had been signed on as the regular minstrel clippies, to sing the Bus songs and tell the pedestrians some of what was happening inside the Bus. Other specific stimuli were provided — for example, the 'Lullaby to a Baby Bus' might be sung to a miniature bus swaddled in the arms of one of the clippies. The fun spilled out on the street, and, in an accumulation of activities, disarmed people of any inhibitions they might have about entering this weird transport. They wanted to get involved. The Kinetic Window Boxes were particularly apt motivators: even while they were still outside, the audience could see some of the fun going on inside.

THE PASSENGERS' BUS

The moment somebody climbs on board the Fun Art Bus, the moment they become a passenger, Street Theatre locks tightly into Environmental Theatre.*
As Ed sees it, Environmental Theatre is of two kinds, which he refers to as the pure and the bastard. The pure form operates within a specific environment, the bastard form in a neutral environment. A neutral environment — it may be a hall, a playground or even a theatre — is one used as a container for another assumed environment such as would not spring immediately to mind in the given location. A café, for instance, can be used in the context of both forms: either as a café (the specific environment), or as a place in which something that is not a café — it might be a bank or a country glade — is reproduced. In the same way a street can be used to show people what it is/could be like to be in a street, or for putting on Shakespeare, as Joseph Papp and his Mobile Theater have demonstrated with questionable success in New York. However, pure environmentalism, particularly when fun is provided as a key element, has its limitations in the street: to remain true to its purpose it would have to accommodate one of the overwhelming qualities of streets — hostility — to make its impact. The Bus, because it inherently contains so many other qualities, avoids this contagion.

As a real environment the Bus provides a form or set of forms which passengers can immediately recognize as a distinct aspect of their everyday experience, and which therefore they have no difficulty in understanding; this was important because one of the functions of the Bus is to bring entertainment to people who do not necessarily have much knowledge of the conventions of the ordinary theatre. Also most of us go out of our way to avoid unfamiliar situations. Further, what is a ready-made low-key experience — travelling on a bus — is eminently suitable for dramatic distortion in terms of sounds, sights and people.

The upsetting of the usual, which begins outside the Bus, continues inside. The juxtaposition and reversal of outdoor and indoor values constitute the keys to the design and fixtures. Looking out of the back window at the bottom of the stairs one is confronted with, in place of the usual pane of window glass, four distinct country scenes surrounded by lace curtains; these are composed of jig-saw pieces, with just a sufficient number of these pieces missing to suggest that the gaps are intentional. The luggage rack beneath the stairs contains its own country scene: it is hoped that in the middle of the city you have come face to

*Ed Berman's long essay on Environmental Theatre, on which the following is based, will form the preface to the edition of his early plays, SAGITTARIUS and VIRGO, to be published in Methuen Playscripts.

29

face with the luggage of your mind — there is an effective literalism beneath the artistic conceit. And so on, up to the painted sky at the top of the cosy cottage staircase. The theme of reversal (of expectations as much as anything else) is continued in other dimensions. It is echoed, for example, in a piece of music that Mike Gibbs put together for the Bus: taking a tape of an earlier recorded piece, he cut it up into inch-long sections and then, completely at random, stuck them together again; this assemblage is played through, and then played backwards. Again, when you receive the Self Illustrating Post Card on the way out, you are handed a passive image where perhaps you had expected an active one. As Ed put it, actually to send it to anyone would be like sending postcards from a Beethoven concert: travelling on the Bus is not an experience that can be photographed.

Because of the built-in realism of the Bus, nothing done on it could be too absurd. The design, whatever its elements, does no more than modify an actual environment; and because of this common limitation the artistic inputs automatically tend to harmonize. There is literally no room for pretension. Pigs must have wings if they are to fly: on the Fun Art Bus passengers can actually climb the staircase, and not just look at it.

THE SMALLEST CINEMA ON WHEELS

In the sense of using materials not specifically created for the Bus, the cinema was the only let-off. This was mainly a matter of finance and a lack of time in which Inter-Action could make its own films — the available resources were concentrated on the video-system. There is of course no reason why such films should not be made in the future, either by Inter-Action or by anybody else with the right idea. As it was, the gap was filled by a number of donations, most of them exclusive: Bob Godfrey and the Animation Department of the West Surrey College of Art provided the Bus with Kevin Attew's 'Tension', 'Goldilocks' (animated by M. P. Rhodes and read by Susan Crabbe), 'The Dong with the Luminous Nose' (M. P. Rhodes, read by Peter Meyer), and 'Mr Slater's Paris' (music by the Bonzo Dog Doo-Dah Band); John Hallas of the E.F.C. lent a print of Gerald Hoffnung's celebrated 'Vacuum Cleaner'; while 'Cameraman' (John Beech and the Polytechnic of Central London), 'Bob Kerr's Whoopee Band' (Alan Moore and Bob Godfrey), and the 'Bus Sub-Scene' (Paul Wilks), a delightful study of a woman's legs crossing and uncrossing in a public place, were donated directly by their creators.

The films were back-projected. Behind the same screen there is also a slide-projector. For the first season Ian Breakwell sent in a pack of slides entitled 'Yes/No', a series of linearly developed images taking a close look at the mouth. Another sequence, composed of photographs of London at its most unflattering by Rod Morrison, provided the visual accompaniment for Ed's 'City Ditty':

Battery chicken
Battery hen
Battery children
Battery men
Battery, batteried, battering, battered
Higgledy-piggledy, cowering, scattered

31

Batteried mind
Batteried soul
Batteried cipher
Batteried whole
Battery, batteried, battering, battered
Higgledy-piggledy, cowering, scattered

Battering women
Battering backs
Battering victims
Battering blacks
Battery, batteried, battering, battered
Higgledy-piggledy, cowering, scattered

Battery chicken
Battery hen
Battery children
Battery men
Battery, batteried, battering, battered
Higgledy-piggledy, cowering, scattered

Batteried mind
Batteried soul
Batteried cipher
Batteried whole
Battery, batteried, battering, battered
Higgledy-piggledy, cowering, scattered.

THE CLOSED-CIRCUIT TELEVISION

A great amount of material was accumulated for the video-system, but unfortunately, for temporary technical reasons, none of it was used more than once during the first season. However it is expected that the system will be put to full use in the future. In practice the tendency was in any case to focus as much attention as possible on the live shows on the top deck; although this obviously placed the actors under greater strain than they had expected, it provided a richer situation for the audience.

3: The Theatre on the Upper Deck

The environmental nature of the Bus is crucial to the theatrical activities which are the core of the participatory entertainment offered by the Bus. There is a freedom — as it was found during the first season — to develop forms of drama that are not confronted with the familiar problem of relating the audience to the situation. As Jim Hiley put it, every member of the audience is involved by simply being there in the Bus. De rigeur, there is a strong attachment to face and face-to-face values. And because the audience are seeing things in a context they are not used to seeing them in, their expectations are minimized, and therefore the possibility of entertaining them maximized. This is not an artistic volte face, but rather a way of asserting the premium placed upon audience enjoyment as a real purpose of theatrical activity, as well as a means of over-coming the limitation of time which is circumstantially forced upon each trip. Again, the fact that on most trips the players have already introduced them-selves to the audience on the street means that there is a degree of intimacy even before a show begins. The net result of all this is that it is relatively easy to attain a speedy 'high'. It is significant that among the very few people who have seemed to get little or nothing out of travelling on the Bus are those avid theatre-goers who, having read or heard about it, deliberately sought it out, rather than allowing it to find them.

There is obviously little room for scenery in the tiny stage area at the front end of the top deck. The only regular prop is a short bench placed beneath the front windows, which are boarded up like the rest. The proscenium arch has two functions: principally it is a joke, in keeping with the absurdity of the overall design; it also serves as a test barrier between players and passengers, particularly in the sense that it can be ignored. In the work done so far, much of the acting has taken place in the aisle, and members of the audience, children especially, have had no hesitations about encroaching on what is formally the stage.

The Other Company and the Dogg's Troupe, working separately, together make up the Bus Company. They are two very different combinations, with distinct traditions. The Dogg's Troupe is Ed's own pet, reared to spearhead Inter-Action's community drive, specializing in Street and participatory theatre, especially for children, with an accumulation of musical and other skills. TOC is a more formal drama group, built up by Naftali Yavin, with Ed and providing the acting quorum for the Almost Free Theatre. Although their dissimilarities are not rigid, their contributions are presented separately.

FROM THE BUS REPERTOIRE

There was a repertoire of shorter pieces and sketches by a variety of writers which was available to any company performing on the Bus. The repertoire provided fill-ins and alternatives to the longer shows, and a selection is given before reviewing the work performed independently by the Dogg's Troupe and The Other Company. Originally intended for the video system, Jim Hiley's *How To Travel in Fun and Comfort* exploits bathetically the vernacular of space-age travel. Conversation pieces, like Michael Stevens' *We're All Going To Southampton*, or situational confrontations like Chris Bailey's *Strong Right Arm Stuff*, could, with minimum adaptation, be performed almost anywhere that provides a setting for the casual encounter. And a delightfully terse dialogue between the sexes, *An Amour* by David Halliwell, could not only be performed anywhere, but almost anyhow, as the companies found out in rehearsal.

How To Travel In Fun And Comfort
by Jim Hiley

This is designed to be delivered by a neatly uniformed STEWARDESS with a plastic smile and that plastic voice that's not giving away how many times she's done it before.

Good afternoon, ladies and gentlemen; London Transport welcomes you aboard this ultra-modern vehicle, Tardis. During most of the journey, we will be travelling at a height of six inches above the ground; for those of you in the upper saloon . . . seven feet six inches. The weather is fine, but we expect it to be pretty disgusting by the time you reach your desination. We'll be travelling at speed if the lights fall in our favour.

At take-off there will be a signal . . . ping-ping.

(She says it straight and mimes pulling the bell-cord twice.)

For safety reasons, you are asked to grip firmly on to the person in front of you. Passengers in the front seats should strap themselves securely into their raincoats. Please place all hand-baggage above your heads. This is essential. We apologize for the delay in providing luggage-racks, and trust that passengers will co-operate by using their arms.

During the journey, passengers will be served with a typical native 'Cockney' dish of Wimpey The Pure Beef Beefburger and baked beans. These will reach you in hygenically dehydrated 'mini-packs' one inch square. Passengers not carrying a supply of water are asked to reconstitute their meals by spitting on them like this.

(She spits twice in a gentile way.)

Passengers are reminded that spitting is prohibited. A varied selection of cigarettes is to be found . . . on the floor. Passengers are reminded that smoking is prohibited.

For mothers with small children, their offspring can be locked up in the cupboard under the stairs, and their screams heard only by those travelling economy class. Should you be taken ill during the journey, recepticles are provided in the pockets of adjacent passengers. Ahead of you is a streamlined individual lavatory, which comes to you in three dimensions and is operated by pulling the chain. As an alternative fully air-conditioned toilet facilities are to be found on the roof. Please do not use the roof while the bus is passing high-rise buildings or rounding sharp corners. In case of accident, this vehicle is fitted with an emergency exit at the rear. However, passengers who are more than twelve inches wide are advised to use the stairs.

A choice of entertainment is provided throughout the journey. In the upper saloon, the Light Opera Society of London Transport Employees presents gems from *The Gondoliers*; in the lower saloon, our Route Inspector will personally execute ten taxi drivers and assorted motorists.

And now I'm going to read a message from our driver, Captain Hannibal Lucky O'Toole: 'Will the little bugger over my head stop kicking the floor'. We hope that you enjoy your journey, and arrive at your destination before the end of the present shift.

Good luck.

(END)

ACT

by James Saunders

Characters: MAN
               FRIEND

MAN: I'd like your attention please while my friend performs a remarkable feat which he is going to perform. Can I have attention!

(Pause.)

We are fortunate tonight to have with us a man who might well have been somewhere else had it not been for various circumstances, who has consented to enter into the spirit of the occasion by performing his remarkable feat on account of which he will undoubtedly become famous in the future as indeed he would already be if not for the ignorance and bigotry of the world of science, notoriously hidebound in its thinking and esconced in its own preconceptions. Are you ready? (To FRIEND.)

Let me make it clear that my friend performs for no reasons of vanity or personal aggrandisement. Public acclaim is of no interest to him. He takes no credit for his remarkable gift any more than he does for the accident of birth which has set his left ear, if you will observe, slightly higher than the other. He performs for the public good, to help breach as he would put it the walls of the prison of ignorance within which our materialistic society and its lackeys the so-called scientists would have us confronted. You're not doing it yet are you? No, he's not doing it yet.

I should like to add at the risk of embarrassing my friend who is as I have said a modest man, that in addition to his particular gift he is the possessor of a profound and original mind the depths of which I have only begun to plumb. This is not the place for a detailed analysis of his extraordinary and far-reaching, I might say world-shattering ideas, even were I capable of it, which I am not. However, one shall I say spin-off from that unfettered brain might help you appreciate the implications of the feat he is to perform.

This is his conviction that Western science, by slavishly obeying the dictum that every phenomenon must demonstrate its existence, has walled us up in a materialistic tomb. 'Let us shake off the dead hand of twentieth century pseudo-scientific clap-trap' cries my friend; 'Everything exists unless you can prove it doesn't.' But enough of that. Shall we start? (To FRIEND.)

Before my friend performs the actual feat, an introductory word is necessary. Don't misunderstand me, this is no showman's trick to create false suspense to bolster up a second-class act. Not at all, his feat speak for themselves; his speat — his feat speaks for itself. However, such is the stranglehold with which the high priests of materialism hold in thrall the mind of modern man that for those unwilling or unable to break through their intellectual cocoons the audacious effect to be witnessed in a moment may well appear in a false light, or even not appear at all, so a word of warning is in order. Indeed, when I was first confronted with this phenomenon which would baffle all the so-called scientists of England if they would but take rock of it, which they won't, I too saw nothing. My friend is now removing his clothes. But the scales fell from my eyes. I persuaded my friend that his gift must be used for the betterment of mankind, to prove once and for all that man is sinking into a quagmire of his own making. Alas, as I said, science has chained itself to a rock and fights off its would-be rescuer with cries of fraud and paranoia. Very well, then, we shall attack the grass roots, appeal to the layman who, conditioned though he may be, is not immured in vested interest. The disrobing has no lascivious intent, but is purely for enhancement of the effect. Observe in fact that my friend retains the underpants, not out of prudery but for reasons to be explained in a moment. My friend is ready. Ladies and gentlemen, my friend will now make himself disappear. are you ready? (To FRIEND.)

(Looks at watch.)

While my friend focuses his will upon a task which our quota of scientific mentors would with one voice condemn as impossible in spite of evidence to the contrary in the writings of the ancients, let me explain how I came to be associated with this remarkable man. I had been sitting for some time one day in the waiting room of a veterinary surgeon, a slow old man and a complete idiot like most doctors, veterinary and otherwise, who died not long afterwards. Suddenly I realized that for some minutes something had been troubling me, some disturbance in the ether. I turned. On the bench alongside me sat my friend, at that time a stranger to me. He had a little dog on his lap and was as he is now, quite still, a figure of inactivity. 'What are you doing?' I asked him. He seemed not at all surprised by my question. 'I'm making myself disappear' he answered. I decided to make a joke of it. 'You're not very good at it, are you?' 'I am' was the reply, 'I'm perfect.' 'But I can still see you' I said. 'No you can't.' 'But I can.' 'You can't.' 'I can.' This went on for some time until we both fell silent. My friend is now invisible.

It was not until five or ten minutes later that he turned to me again, touched my shoulder and said: 'It's in your mind.' 'What?' 'It's in your imagination. You saw me when you came in and knew I was still here so you assumed you could still see me. The power of imagination.' 'But' I said, 'I can hear you speak.' 'Well, I'm speaking.' 'But your lips are moving.' 'Imagination' he said. I stared at him. 'It's no good staring' he said, 'I'm back now.' I was flabbergasted. 'It's true' he said. 'You can't disprove it.' 'What about the little dog?' I asked; 'Does he disappear too?' 'Of course not' he said; 'Dogs can't do it.' 'Are you still invisible?'

(The FRIEND says 'Yes', but soundlessly.)

My friend is now bringing this demonstration to its culmination by dressing while still invisible. You will appreciate now the reason for the retaining of the underpants. Actual nudity is one thing; the grotesque projection of a febrile imagination quite another, with possible traumatic consequences.

FRIEND: I'm not having Tom, Dick and Harry sketching in my private parts. You don't know what they'd get up to.

MAN: Are you back?

FRIEND: Of course I'm back.

MAN: I can't see you.

FRIEND: Your imagination again. Come on, I'm sick of this.

(Exit.)

(END)

Strong Right Arm Stuff

By Chris Bailey

Characters: FRANK
            NEB

So there's a man sitting on a moving bus. Call him FRANK.
Keeping himself very much to himself.
Seat to himself and spread over it slightly to
discourage others from sitting next to him.

Another man, call him NEB, comes up the bus stairs
with an imaginary very large dog, on a lead.
Small, with a weak (piping or maybe a stutter) voice.
Not camp.

He goes down the bus. Frightened of people, as he so
much as brushes the clothing of passengers he passes
he says Sorry, or Scuse.

Stands at FRANK's seat, waiting for FRANK to move across
and make room for him. FRANK doesn't.

The dog only exists for NEB, and maybe not for him.

NEB: Scuse . . . Scuse. Sorry.

Could you shift up a bit d'you
think?

(FRANK does so grudgingly.)

NEB: Sorry.

FRANK: Salright.

NEB: Sorry.
I didn't catch what you said.

FRANK: Nothing.

NEB: Oh right.

(NEB gets comfortable, staring at FRANK.)

FRANK: Who you staring at?

NEB: Does the dog worry you?
There's no need. Honest. (Authorative shout.)
SIT. YOU GREAT BONE HEADED HOUND
YOU.
He gets edgy in company.
That's all. Nothing to worry about.
Not so long as I'm here.
I'm his master see.
I'm training him.

FRANK: No kid.

NEB: Oh yes. You can take my word.
He's under control.

FRANK: Alright go on then. I'll buy it.

NEB: How d'you mean?

FRANK: Whatever it is.

NEB: TONGUE OUT.
There see.
It's all in the tone of voice you
use. You've got to be firm.
That's the secret with these.
Training see.
PUT YOUR TONGUE IN, YOU STUPID
SLAVERING SLOB.
Even teach it manners eh!
(To DOG:) NOW BEHAVE.
He knows what he'll get if he
doesn't. No doubt of that.
He's had it before.

FRANK (very conscious of being in limelight and not liking it):
Put a sock in it will you.

NEB: Sorry.

(Pause whilst FRANK looks out of the window.
Not quite sure, but almost that he's been landed with
a nutter. And people are watching.
NEB's too full of it to be quiet long.)

NEB: No like I say.
The thing with these.
Train them properly you've
got a friend for life.
More than you can say for some
people anyway.
. . . Innit?
He answers only to me.
I mean take you for instance.
Big and strong as you are.
You could order him til the cows
came home and he wouldn't move
a muscle.
I guarantee it.

FRANK (sarcastic to gallery):
Is that right.

NEB: Tell you what.
Give him an order. Test him out.
You'll see I'm right.
Pass the time won't it. (Reaches out and touches FRANK.)
Go on.

FRANK: Look. Once and for all.
I don't know what it is you're
on. But whatever it is.
You're getting up my nose.
Now just keep it out right. Before
I lose my temper.

NEB: I don't follow.

FRANK: You and me both.
Now I'm telling you.

NEB (timid and hurt):
I thought you were interested.
Sorry.

FRANK: Who is this tit.

NEB: AND WHAT ARE YOU LOOKING AT YOU OVERSIZED
UNDERLING YOU.
Scuse me.

(Reaches out to touch FRANK's sleeve. Thinks better of it.)

NEB: Scuse me.

FRANK: What!

39

NEB: Er . . . Just a word in your ear
  really. A warning.

FRANK: Yeah!

NEB: It's nothing.
  Only. It's not wise. Not raising
  your voice the way you did.
  Not like that.

FRANK: And how's that?

NEB: I'm just saying. The thing I
  didn't mention.
  He's very loyal to me.
  I mean if I was to give him the
  word.
  He'd gnaw your head off. Quick as
  winking. No messing.

  (FRANK rising to the threat.)

FRANK: Well praps —

NEB: Don't get me wrong.
  He never gets carried away.
  Protecting me . . . well it's in his
  training.
  That's why I got him. Protection.
  Not from people like you.
  There'd be no need. You're a reasonable
  man.
  But let's suppose I'm on the bus
  top deck. Late night. On my tod.
  And there's these three youths.
  Off the leash. Looking for trouble.
  Untrained let's say.
  Well I know it's just high spirits
  to them but it's aching, puking and
  spitting blood to me innit.
  But not any longer. I'm protected.

FRANK: Lucky old you.

NEB: You'll see my point.
  People can be very surprising.
  In my experience.
  I mean picture it.
  Now for instance. I could lean over.
  Casual as you like. To all the world
  looking out of the window.
  And quick one two straight to
  the kidneys.
  People do you know. All the time.

FRANK: Highly likely.

NEB: It happened.

FRANK: Not to me.

NEB: Anyway now I'm alert to all that.

(Suddenly FRANK's thought of a way of coping with an increasingly embarrassing situation.)

FRANK: All right set it on.

NEB: Eh.

FRANK: Now. On me.
. . . Why don't you.

NEB: Why?

FRANK: Does it matter.
Maybe I've got a taste for it.
You don't know do you?
. . . Come on then . . .
What are we waiting for?

NEB: It's not so —

FRANK: After all you could call it off
before it's gnawed my head *right*
off.

NEB: You don't know what you're
asking.

FRANK: Oh yes I do mate. Exactly.
And so do you.
Now come on. (Bares his throat.)
Unleash it.

NEB' I can't.

FRANK: And why's that I ask myself.

NEB: You must understand —

FRANK: I do.

NEB: It's me is responsible.
Yes I could only see my way
clear . . . in situations fraught . . .
with great personal danger.
And . . . then. In an emergency.

FRANK: Set it on.
You've got a count of three.
One.

NEB: I know what it's like . . .

FRANK: Two.

NEB: To be hurt in public.

More than anything else.
The embarrassment of it. I wouldn't wish
that on anybody.

FRANK: Right.

(Punches him hard in the stomach.
Hard. NEB doubles up.)

FRANK: Sorry.

(Curtain or whatever.)

(END)

We're All Going To Southampton

by Michael Stevens

Characters: WALTER
           DEREK
           CONDUCTOR

A man is sitting on the bus. Quite an old man. A younger man gets on and sits next to him. Very abruptly the conversation begins.

WALTER (the older man): What's your mother's name?

DEREK (the younger man): Sorry?

WALTER: What's your mother's name?

DEREK: You mean her Christian name?

WALTER (more aggressively): What's her name? Your mother. What's your mother's name?

DEREK: Jean.

WALTER: My mother's name is Anne.

DEREK: My grandmother's name is Anne.

(Pause. DEREK turns his attention away from WALTER, hoping to avoid any further conversation.)

WALTER: Have you ever been to Paris?

DEREK: Yes.

WALTER (confidentially): There's a train leaves Paris twice a day.

DEREK: For England?

WALTER (contemptuously): For Moscow. It goes via Bremen.

DEREK: Bremen. Germany.

WALTER: I was in Bremen, the Hotel, and Fritz, d'you know how much Fritz charged me for two boiled eggs?

DEREK: No.

WALTER (confidentially): The equivalent of eighteen shillings.

DEREK: When was this?

WALTER (shortly): What?

DEREK: When was this? Before the war?

WALTER (contemptuously again): No. Three days ago. You know the language they speak in East Germany and West Germany, it's not the same language.

DEREK: Oh? I thought it was.

WALTER: No. Never has been. Do you know 'Nein' in German?

DEREK: Yes.

WALTER: D'you know what it means?

DEREK: Nein?

WALTER: Yes.

DEREK: 'No'.

WALTER: What?

DEREK: It means 'No'.

WALTER: No.

DEREK: Yes.

WALTER: No it doesn't.

DEREK (getting involved): D'you mean 'Nein' in German or 'Nine' in English?

WALTER: 'Nein'.

DEREK: 'Neun'.

WALTER: What?

DEREK: 'Nine' is 'Neun'.

WALTER: No.

DEREK: It is. Neun. 'Neun' is 'Nine'. 'Neun' the German word 'Neun' means 'nine' in English. 'Neun' is 'nine'.

WALTER (confidentially): 'Nein' means 'naughty'.

(DEREK realizes more the situation.)

DEREK: I see.

WALTER: You've got your 'O' Levels and your 'A' Levels I suppose.

DEREK: What?

WALTER: You've got your 'O' Levels and your 'A' Levels I suppose.

DEREK: Yes.

WALTER: Then tell me.

DEREK: Yes?

WALTER: Why do you go about Cambridge with no shoes on?

DEREK: I never have.

WALTER: Only tramps do that. I'm going tonight.

DEREK: To Cambridge?

WALTER (with scorn): No! To Nova Scotia. Canada. I'm going to Southampton first. To meet a fellow. I rang him up this morning. Well, he rang me up. He's got everything fixed up. He told me not to get there before seven.

DEREK: Well, you've plenty of time. Are you going by bus?

WALTER: What?

DEREK: Are you going by bus?

WALTER: No! I've got a car. Down the road. Against Nellie's. Do you know Nellie?

DEREK: No.

WALTER: Married Reece. A Welshman. Do you know David?

DEREK: Is he Welsh?

WALTER: No! He lives in Salisbury. On the Wiltshire Downs. He came from Northumberland. Tokyo's a beautiful city.

DEREK: Yes.

WALTER: And Hong Kong. It used to be British.

DEREK: Yes.

WALTER: I know why you're here.

DERRK: Oh yes?

WALTER (confidentially again): You're down from Leicester. After the judies.

DEREK: Yes. You're right.

WALTER: They can't sell New Zealand.

DEREK: No. (Humouring him.) It's too expensive.

(Pause.)

WALTER: What is?

DEREK: New Zealand.

WALTER: New Zealand?

DEREK (trying to explain): Too expensive. To sell. New Zealand. (Lamely.) If you wanted to sell it.

WALTER: If you wanted to sell New Zealand???

DEREK: Yes.

WALTER: You don't know what you're talking about.

DEREK: I said . . .

WALTER: Yes?

DEREK: I said . . . you said they can't sell New Zealand.

WALTER: I never.

44

DEREK: You . . .

WALTER: You said it was too expensive.

DEREK: Yes.

WALTER: Where are you going?

DEREK: Me?

WALTER: On this bus. Where are you going?

DEREK: . . .

WALTER: It's not going to . . .

DEREK: It's not.

WALTER: No.

DEREK: It's going to Tokyo!

WALTER (aggressively): What?

DEREK: Where's it going?

WALTER: This bus is going to Southampton. We're all going to Southampton. Have you ever been to Plymouth?

DEREK: No.

WALTER: We're all going.

DEREK: Yes.

WALTER: To Southampton.

DEREK: Yes.

WALTER: So remember.

DEREK: Yes.

CONDUCTOR: Mersey Tunnel!

WALTER: This is where I get off. Remember.

DEREK: Yes.

(END)

Bus Trip

by Frank Marcus

Characters: MAN
            GIRL
            YOUTH
            STRANGER

Two parallel seats are reversed and face the passengers on the top deck, turning them into spectators. A MAN and a GIRL occupy the two window seats. He is

45

the 'City Gent' type — or at least aspires to be one. She is twentyish, sleepy, and vapid.

MAN: Made it. Jolly good effort. Out of breath. Dearie me. Near thing.

GIRL: I wish I could have stayed in bed.

MAN: All bright and cheerful. Crisp. Ready — nay, willing — to face the challenges, ardours, anxieties, tribulations, terrors of Amplifex Limited. (Looking out of the window.) If the number of lamp-posts we count before we stop at traffic lights exceeds 25, it'll be a good omen.

GIRL: Plugging in, plugging out. That's all it amounts to. 'Being a telephonist provides you with golden opportunities for promotion: you are the nerve-centre of activities.' Pardon me if I try a bitter laugh. (She does so.)

(A YOUTH hurries up the gangway and sits next to the GIRL.)

YOUTH: Was that a smile of encouragement? There's lots of seats — she must be wondering why I chose to sit next to her. I'll try giving her one of those sideway looks.

GIRL: Oh, Gawd. Another one in search of a top-deck romance. I hope he doesn't turn out to be a groper . . .

MAN: Twenty-three, twenty-four, twenty-five. Hurrah! Done it!! (Deflated.) Done what?

GIRL: That slimey character last week who pretended his small change had fallen out of his pocket and slipped under my bottom and started looking for it . . .

YOUTH: Opening gambit. Neutral remark about the weather? Complaints about the traffic? General comments about life? Catch her eye and give an encouraging smile? One of those cheeky, but goodnatured smiles?

(He tries to catch her eye, but she stares determinedly out of the window.)

MAN: I hope I don't bump into Miss Wilkinson on the way in. Seeing her first thing casts a sort of blight over the whole week. They say she's been disappointed a lot, she's had a hard life . . . Sour old bitch.

YOUTH: Christ, you get more response from a dead fish.

GIRL: I like maturity in a man.

(Eccentrically dressed, singing 'Hi, ho, it's off to work we go', and skipping in rhythm to it, the STRANGER arrives and sits next to the MAN.)

STRANGER: Hello, hello, hello. Mornin' all. Happy and cheerful, are we?

MAN: He *would* have to sit next to me.

YOUTH: A nut-case.

STRANGER: How about champagne for breakfast? That's the way to start in style, eh? (He mimes uncorking a bottle of champagne and imagines it gushing out. To GIRL.) Haven't spilled any over your dress, have I?

GIRL: No, that's quite all right. (To herself.) What did I say that for? I'm daft, that's what.

STRANGER (handing an imaginary glass to the YOUTH): Drink up, young man.

YOUTH (accepting the imaginary glass): It's best to humour them. Ta.

STRANGER: Cheers. (Speaking as one expert to another, to the MAN.) Veuve Clicquot 1947. Nothing to beat it. (The MAN strenuously ignores him.) Not thirsty. Come along, you can't fool me – you don't have the look of a tea-totaller.

MAN (looking frantic): Where's the conductor? Can't even ride on a bus without being molested.

STRANGER: A little music? (To the YOUTH.) What's your favourite instrument?

YOUTH: The bass guitar.

STRANGER (to the GIRL): Any favourite tune?

GIRL (embarrassed): No, thank you.

(STRANGER mimes strumming a guitar.)

MAN (desperately): Please, someone, take him away.

(The sound of a loud bang, possibly a burst tyre, enables the STRANGER to mime that the guitar has exploded.)

STRANGER: Here's a pretty kettle of fish. (He fans imaginary smoke and coughs.) So sorry for the inconveneince. Faulty wiring. (To the YOUTH.) Let me try to get the stain off your jacket. (He rubs the YOUTH's elbow.)

YOUTH (sheepishly grinning): That's all right. Don't mind me.

STRANGER (to the GIRL): Are you in any way damaged, Miss? May I examine . . . ?

YOUTH (shielding her): Come off it, mate.

STRANGER (catching sight of the MAN, screams): Your face has gone black!

MAN (temporarily unsettled): Where! What . . . ?

STRANGER: Aha, caught you.

MAN: Look here –

STRANGER (rising, and grabbing a rope): Tug 'o war. Come on. Cheer me on. You're in my team, you know. (He mimes a tug 'o war, pulling and being pulled strenuously.) Come on, pull. All of you. You're not making enough effort. You're leaving it all to me. (He mimes being pulled out of sight.) Going, going . . . (He disappears.)

MAN (relieved): Well, thank God for that!

GIRL: Never know who you're going to come across these days.

YOUTH: He was nutty, he was. But harmless with it.

MAN: I'm not so sure. They let them all out these days, they used to keep them locked up.

GIRL: Yes, it's not right.

YOUTH (anxious to agree with her): No, it's not right.

MAN: Bit of an adventure, eh? I thought we handled it pretty well.

GIRL: Yes, we soon got rid of him.

MAN (to YOUTH): You bore the brunt, I'm afraid.

YOUTH: Oh, that's all right.

GIRL (to YOUTH): It was nice of you not to let him —

YOUTH: Well, I couldn't, could I?

GIRL: Anyway, thanks a lot.

MAN: Not every day you come across . . . (Taking out a packet of cigarettes and offering them) Cigarette?

GIRL: No, thanks. Gave it up last year.

YOUTH (accepting it): I wish I was determined enough —

GIRL: It's easy once you get over the first few days.

YOUTH: I'll take your word for it.

GIRL: I take chewing gum instead. (Offering a packet.) Would you like — ?

YOUTH (helping himself): Thanks. I'll keep it for later.

MAN (declining politely): No, thanks. Gets into my teeth. (An idea occurs to him.) May I ask whether you both work near here?

YOUTH: I get off at the next stop.

GIRL: So do I.

MAN: So do I. What a coincidence! Might I suggest, if it's no imposition, that you join me for a drink at the Duke of Argyll's at lunchtime? You know where it is?

GIRL: Thanks. That'll be lovely.

YOUTH: Super.

MAN: I think we deserve a little celebration.

(The STRANGER's voice is heard approaching, calling, 'Ices, Cones or Tubs. Chocolate or Vanilla.' He comes on, walking backwards, serving imaginary cones to children.)

STRANGER: Seven new pence. Thank you. Mind how you hold it. Look out — it's dropping!

MAN (aghast): Oh, no!!

STRANGER (to MAN): Feel like a game of table tennis? My turn to serve. (He mimes a game of table tennis.) Fifteen-Love.

(The MAN, the YOUTH, and the GIRL flee.)

STRANGER (calling after them): Care for a dance, Miss? (He dances briefly.) I say, young man. Your turn. (He mimes hairdressing.) Just a bit of trimming, eh? A bit of thinning out? Yes, the days of 'short back and sides' are over, aren't they? Can't say I regret them. Shampoo? Scalp massage? (Holding an invisible mirror at the back of his customer's haead.) All right? Nice, neat line. Observe the curve in the nape of the neck. (Accepting a tip.) Thank you. Anything else you require? Good afternoon, Sir. The next gentleman, please. Nobody? Nobody at all? (Gruffly.) Oh, all right then. (He sits down and plays a mimed game of patience.) Solitaire. That's French for alone.

(END)

SHURRUP

by Henry Livings

Characters: GIRL
                MAN

A GIRL enters to sit on the bench, with an open paper bag in which there is a banana. She looks round, and nods to us in fresh appreciation of the venue. Sets the bag by her.

A MAN enters and chooses to sit by her; he is also pleased with the spot and with us, when he's considered it.

The GIRL absently reaches to the bag for the banana.

His attention attracted, the MAN screws himself down to see what her dainty fingers are reaching after. Finds out.

MAN (to us): She's got a banana.

    (She glances at him; decides to leave the banana lying there.)

MAN: Can I hold it?

GIRL: What?

MAN: Can I hold your banana?

    (She can't think why not.)

GIRL: All right; if you want to.

    (He holds the banana.)

GIRL: Hey no, give it me back. (Grabs it.)

MAN: Are you going to be eating it in a minute?

GIRL: Yes.

MAN: Can I watch?

GIRL: Shurrup.

MAN: I want to watch.

GIRL: I said shurrup.

MAN: You're going to eat it aren't you. You're going to peel it, and then eat it.

    (Affecting indifference, she peels down the top half.)

MAN: Oh my heavens.

GIRL: Shurrup watching, d'you hear me.

MAN: You could just lick it.

49

GIRL: I will not just lick it.

MAN: You could though.

GIRL: Shurrup.

MAN: Or you could suck it.

GIRL: Shurrup!

MAN: If you sucked it it'd last longer. (Concentrated.) Are you going to eat it?

GIRL: *Yes.* (She bites a bit off.)

MAN: Reckless.

GIRL (bites a bit more): You what?

MAN: Oh my heavens that's half of it gone: there'll be teeth marks.

GIRL: I've a good mind not to eat this damn banana.

MAN (anxious): You can't stop now.

(Tentatively, and with several glances towards him, she ingorges the remainder. He groans with empathetic, quiet enjoyment, hypnotized.)

GIRL: Shurrup will you; I've eaten my banana, and I'm damn going.

MAN: Yes, yes, I understand.

GIRL (going): You're daft you.

MAN: Hey! tomorrow . . .

GIRL: What?

MAN: Tomorrow would you bring a cream horn?

(She flounces off, a little warm.)

MAN (replete): Oh my heavens; it's better than a hot dinner.

(Goes, giving one little skip.)

(END)

An Amour

by David Halliwell

Characters: MAN
            WOMAN

A young MAN and WOMAN sitting on a long seat. They sit with as much space between them as possible. Both wear heavy overcoats.

MAN: Ey.

(Silence.)

MAN: Ey.

(Silence.)

MAN: Ey you!

WOMAN: Wot?

MAN: A lov y'.

WOMAN: Y' wot?

MAN: A lov y'.

WOMAN: Y wot?

MAN: A sed A lov y'.

WOMAN: Wot d' y' meen?

MAN: A meen A lov y'.

WOMAN: 'Ow d' y' meen?

MAN: A meen A bluddy well lov y'.

WOMAN: A don't know wot y' meen?

MAN: A meen A bluddy well lov y'.

WOMAN: A don't know wot y' talkin' about.

MAN: A'm talkin' about lovin' y'.

WOMAN: I don't know wot.

MAN: D' y' 'ear wot A'm sayin'?

WOMAN: A don't know.

MAN: D' y' fuckin'-well 'ear wot A'm sayin'.

   (Pause.)

WOMAN: S'pose so.

MAN: Wot?

WOMAN: Well.

MAN: Wot?

WOMAN: Well.

MAN: Wot?

WOMAN: Well.

MAN: Wot?

WOMAN: Well.

MAN: Wot?

WOMAN: Well.

MAN: Wot!

   (Pause.)

WOMAN: Y' lov me.

MAN: Wot?

WOMAN: Y' lov me.

MAN: Right.

(Pause.)

WOMAN: Wot foh?

MAN: 'Ow d' y' meen?

WOMAN: Wot d' y' lov me foh?

MAN: Wot do A lov y' foh?

WOMAN: Aye wot d' y' lov me foh?

MAN: Don't y' know?

WOMAN: No.

MAN: Y' do.

WOMAN: A don't.

MAN: Y' do.

WOMAN: A don't.

MAN: Y've no idea.

WOMAN: No.

MAN: Non at all?

WOMAN: No.

MAN: Y' 'ave.

WOMAN: A've not.

MAN: Y' 'ave.

WOMAN: A've not.

MAN: Well can't y' guess?

WOMAN: No.

MAN: Not at all?

WOMAN: NO.

MAN: Becos y' luvly.

WOMAN: Y' wot?

MAN: Y' luvly.

WOMAN: Y' wot?

MAN: Y' luvly.

WOMAN: Wot d' y' meen?

MAN: A meen y' luvly.

WOMAN: Wot d' y' meen?

MAN: A meen y' bluddy luvly.

WOMAN: 'Ow d' y' meen?

MAN: Well — in y'r appearance.

WOMAN: In me wot?

MAN: In y' luks.

WOMAN: Me luks?

MAN: Aye. Y' face.

WOMAN: Wot face?

MAN: Y' face.

WOMAN: Me face?

MAN: Aye y' face. Don't y' know wot y' face is?

WOMAN: 'Course A do.

MAN: Well it's luvly.

WOMAN: No it in't.

MAN: It is.

WOMAN: It in't.

MAN: It is.

WOMAN: It in't.

MAN: Why not?

WOMAN: A don't know.

MAN: Well I know why it is.

WOMAN: Why?

MAN: Becos' it's oval.

WOMAN: It's not.

MAN: It is.

WOMAN: No.

MAN: Y' can't see it.

WOMAN: A've seen it.

MAN: A'm starin' at it.

WOMAN: A've seen it.

MAN: Well A'm sittin' 'ere starin' at it.

WOMAN: A c'n remember it.

MAN: No y' can't.

WOMAN: 'Course A can.

MAN: Y've forgotten it.

WOMAN: NO A've not.

MAN: Y'can't recall it.

WOMAN: You can't see straight.

MAN: A can see it's oval.

WOMAN: No.

MAN: An' therefore luvly.

WOMAN: No.

MAN: An' it's not t' on'y thing.

WOMAN: T' on'y wot?

MAN: T' on'y thing.

WOMAN: T' on'y thing wot?

MAN: S' not t' on'y thing 'at's luvly.

WOMAN: Wot d' y' meen?

MAN: Well y' figger.

WOMAN: Me wot?

MAN: Y' figger.

WOMAN: 'Ow d' y' meen?

MAN: Well y' tits.

WOMAN: Wot tits?

MAN: Your tits?

WOMAN: Y've never seen 'em.

MAN: I 'ave.

WOMAN: Y' av'nt.

MAN: A've seen where they are.

WOMAN: Where?

MAN: There.

WOMAN: Where?

MAN: On y' front, just below y'r arms.

WOMAN: Y' can't see 'em.

MAN: A can.

WOMAN: Y' can't.

MAN: 'Course A can.

WOMAN: They aren't visible.

MAN: They are.

WOMAN: They arn't.

MAN: T' bulge is.

WOMAN: Wot bulge?

MAN: T' bulge they make.

WOMAN: 'Ow d' y' know it's them.

MAN: 'Ow do A know it's not?

WOMAN: 'Ow d' y' know it's tits?

MAN: Wot else cud it be?

WOMAN: 'O's t' say?

MAN: A growth?

WOMAN: Cud be.

MAN: NO.

WOMAN: 'Ow d' you know?

MAN: A know 'ow y'r formed.

WOMAN: Y' don't.

MAN: A do.

WOMAN: Y' don't.

MAN: Y've tits up there.

WOMAN: Guesswork.

MAN: An' a bum down below.

WOMAN: Y'wot?

MAN: A bum.

WOMAN: A wot?

MAN: A bum, a bottom, an arse.

WOMAN: 'Ow d' y' meen?

MAN: Y' can't deny y've got an arse!

WOMAN: Oo's trying?

MAN: So you'll admit that?

WOMAN: Wot?

MAN: 'at y've got an arse?

WOMAN: S'pose so.

MAN: An' it's luvly.

WOMAN: No.

MAN: Y' wot?

WOMAN: It's not.

MAN: It is! It's — gorgeous.

WOMAN: Y'wot?

MAN: Gorgeous!

WOMAN: It's not.

MAN: It is.

WOMAN: Y've never seen it.

MAN: 'Course I 'ave.

55

WOMAN: 'Ow?

MAN: Throu y' skirt.

WOMAN: 'Ave y' got X ray eyes?

MAN: Course not.

WOMAN: Then 'ow 've y' seen it?

MAN: A've seen 'ow it displaces t' cloth.

WOMAN: That dun't mean owt.

MAN: It doz.

WOMAN: It dun't.

MAN: It meens A've seen y'r arse.

WOMAN: NO.

MAN: An' it's gorgeous.

WOMAN: No.

MAN: It's gorgeous.

WOMAN: It's nout.

MAN: It's magnificent.

WOMAN: It's plain.

MAN: It's excitin'.

WOMAN: It's repulsive.

MAN: It's fantastically excitin'!

WOMAN: No.

MAN: It excites me.

WOMAN: 'Ow d' y' meen?

MAN: A'm cummin' thru me aertex.

WOMAN: Y'r on'y sayin' that becos it's Christmas.

MAN: Chris'mas!

WOMAN: Aye.

MAN: It isn't Chris'mas.

WOMAN: It's November First.

MAN: That's not Christmas.

WOMAN: Well it's neerly Chris'mas.

MAN: Wot duz it matter?

WOMAN: It matters t' me.

MAN: A'd say it any time.

WOMAN: Wot?

MAN: At any time o' t' year.

WOMAN: Wot wud y' say?

MAN: A lov y'.

WOMAN: A don't know wot y' mean.

MAN: Now listen y' stupid bugger.

WOMAN: A don't know wot y'r on about.

MAN: Listen y' stupid bugger.

WOMAN: A don't know wot.

MAN: Listen y' stupid fuckin' bugger!

   (Pause.)

WOMAN: Wot?

MAN: A fuckin' well lov' y'.

WOMAN: Well.

MAN: Wot do A do?

WOMAN: Well.

MAN: Wot do I do?

WOMAN: Y' lov me.

MAN: Right. Why?

WOMAN: A don't know.

MAN: Y' wot?

WOMAN: A don't know.

MAN: A've told y' becos y' luvly.

WOMAN: Y'wot?

MAN: Becos y' bluddy well luvly.

WOMAN: No A'm not.

MAN: You bluddy well are.

WOMAN: No A'm not.

MAN: You fuckin' well are.

WOMAN: No.

MAN: Now listen!

WOMAN: No.

MAN: Listen t' me!

WOMAN: No.

MAN: Listen y' thick bugger!

WOMAN: No.

MAN: Listen or A'll nock y' teeth in!

WOMAN: Well.

MAN: A'll nock y' mis'rable teeth in!

WOMAN: Well.

MAN: A'll nock 'em down y' mawngy throat!

WOMAN: Well.

MAN: Listen y' rancid bitch!

WOMAN: Well.

MAN: Listen y' foul fuckin' cunt!

WOMAN: Well.

MAN: Listen y' stinkin' lumpa shit! Y'r luvly!

   (Black out.)

(END)

THE DOGG'S TROUPE: *'THERE'S NO BUSSINESS LIKE SHOW BUSSINESS'*

Dogg's — Pat Barlow, Katya Benjamin, Bob Hescott, Geoff Hoyle and Ed Berman — performed one show in the first season, Leon Rosselson's *There's No Bussiness Like Show Bussiness*; they later extended their repertoire with a new entertainment written by Chris Bailey, and with a special show for the Bus's visit to the Munich Games. Directed by Noel Grieg, Leon's 'musical hotch-potch' was the first work to be done publicly on the Bus, and was therefore prepared with much care and anxiety.

The show consists of a succession of short sketches and songs in a music-hall revue formula; its open-endedness was ideal for the musical and improvisational skills of the members of the company. Each player in the troupe had his or her own instrument — Pat the guitar, Katya the flute, Bob the saxaphone, Ed, his voice or bugle, and Geoff, in addition to his superb abilities in mime, the violin; together they formed an ensemble that could do virtually anything.

During the third week of rehearsals it was realized that the show lacked a cohesion: each sketch had to stand or fall on its own. This was worrying because, with the Bus still undergoing decoration, nobody knew what would happen when Dogg's finally took to the road: there were simply many unknowns that wouldn't become apparent until the vehicle arrived; not the least of these was whether indeed it would be possible to perform and travel at the same time.

Trusting that whatever the physical hazards might be the show would go on, a solution was found to give it the necessary cement. In the very first rehearsal Noel had posed as an impresario, and taken Dogg's through each sketch as though it were an audition. This condition was now re-imposed: Ed was to be the impresario, riding on the Bus with the passengers dressed in a multi-check suit, acting as ringmaster, goading the players to do something different, something better, something he could sell to the citizens of America: 'I've seen you can sing, what else can you do? . . . The old folk won't like that very much

58

8. *The Electric Piano*

9. *The Dogg's Troupe: Geoff
Hoyle, Pat Barlow, with Ed
Berman in the foreground*

. . . That's nice, but what about something British. I want to see something really British now. You know what I mean by something British, don't you? . . . But that wasn't funny, what about something funny? . . . That's a great idea, I'll buy that.'

A continuous part for an electronic Voice had been written into the original script, issuing instructions and intimidations to the players. This was abandoned because, although Ed trusted his sound system, he didn't want to have to rely on it. In his own way, Ed put the Voice back in, and restored a measure of unity to the show. The ends were tied up by the crass, grasping showman, Otto Premier-Check. Noel was still a little apprehensive about the outcome: wouldn't the audience feel it was being bamboozled into fun? In practice it worked out very differently. Ed always put himself at the back of the deck, thus suspending the passengers in the midst of a confrontation between himself and the other players. If it didn't like something, the audience could share in the impresario's disapproval; and if it enjoyed the routines, then it could join in the players' resentment of Otto Premier-Check. This meant there was no compulsion to enjoy anything, with the result that most passengers enjoyed themselves immensely. It was a way of working inside an audience without appearing to put any pressures on it.

The Bus was ideal for this sort of experiment, and, in Otto Premier-Check's language, the dividends paid off handsomely. In sending the players up, Ed took care to send himself up at the same time, so that he was sufficiently overblown in his role as the protector of the passengers' interests for them not to have to take him seriously.

With Ed's intrusion, *There's No Bussiness Like Show Bussiness* moved steadily away from any scripted form: all the songs were kept, but the intervening dialogue and sketches were only retained in outline, being varied improvisationally according to the age and other characteristics of the audience.

The show opened with a regular Dogg's chorus ('We've Come to Entertain You'), followed by a banana joke (there were several) —

> They call this route the banana route.
> — The banana route?
> The banana route.
> — And why do they call this the banana route?
> (Altogether) Because the buses all come along
> in bunches —

leading straight into the first of Leon's songs:*

> We've played all the buses from Hampstead to Kew,
> From the 12A to Croydon and the seventy two,
> And the seventy four to Earls Court and the Zoo,
> We're the buskers, the buskers, the buskers.
>
> We've played on the eighteen to Paddington Green,
> And we've been out to Enfield on the two seventeen,
> And you'd never believe all the things that we've seen,
> We're the buskers, the buskers, the buskers.

*The music for Leon Rosselson's songs is to be found in the Appendix.

60

We've all served our time on the Red Arrow Line,
We've gone round the Bank on the one forty nine,
With the gents in black bowlers and the Financial Times,
We're the buskers, the buskers, the buskers.

On the two round Hyde Park when the birds are in flower,
And the eighteen to Euston past the Post Office Tower,
And we've sometimes moved two hundred yards in an hour,
We're the buskers, the buskers, the buskers.

Next, two members of the audience were invited to take part in a banana eating contest on, or rather in, the stage:

Can you eat a
Nana neater
that the nana eater
seated next to you?

The bananas were handed up from the controls room, covered with jam, and placed in front of the contestants whose hands were tied behind their backs. Pat was the waitress in this one. In another sketch, 'R. G. Barr Superstar', he played the rock idol:

Hooter's gone,
Clocking on,
Every Monday morning,
On the job,
Turning knobs,
Just a machine.

But watch me on a Saturday,
That's when I make my getaway,
R. G. Barr is on display,
Doing his thing.

And it's R. G. Barr Superstar,
Wizard on the old guitar,
Hear 'em scream,
I'm their dream,
R. G. Barr is King.

la la las . . .

Nine to five,
Just alive,
Monday til Friday,
Turning wheels,
I just feel
I'm a machine.

But Saturday, that's when I'm free,
Rock and Roll in ecstasy,
All the girls wanting me,
R. G. Barr is King.

And it's R. G. Barr, Superstar,
People come from near and far,
Just to see,
Sexy me
Doing my thing.

R. G. Barr, Superstar,
Wizard on the old guitar,
Hear 'em scream,
I'm their dream,
R. G. Barr is King.

If anybody wanted to know, Geoff was ready to show them how to be the
'Tallest Man in the World':

When I was just a little tiny tot,
My father always used to say to me
Walk tall my son, and you'll be ten foot high,
Instead of only being two foot three.

And so
I decided to grow,
Because I knew
That if I grew
I would be — Someone.

They would look up to me because I was someone,
They would admire me because I was someone,
       They couldn't ignore me,
       They would say when they saw me —
(Spoken)   Look at him — he's someone.

Because everyone loves someone
Because everyone loves someone.

At six foot three I said — I can't go on —
Keep trying, son, I heard my father say.
       I tried and tried. Within a week I grew
       Another foot *(waves it)* to help me on my way.

And so
I continued to grow
I was not going to stop
Till I reached the top,
Then I would be
       Someone . . . etc.

And so I rose to fame, I owe it all
To what my father always said to me—
       Walk tall, walk straight and you'll be ten foot high,
       Instead of being only two foot three.

That's how
I got where I am now
And I've always known
That when I was fully grown
I would be −
Someone.

Having successfully explained himself away, Goeff introduced Miss Selena
Sostenuto (Katya) − 'the slinky, seductive, sensuous, sinuous, sensational
artiste de la stripping' − at any rate a take-off of such a person:

Miss Sostenuto, to what do you attribute your
success in the world of nude artistry?
− Jellied Eels.
Jellied Eels?
− My one passion.

And so into Leon's song on the same:

CHORUS: Jellied eels, jellied eels, jumping on the plate,
          Jellied eels, jellied eels, I can hardly wait,
               Jellied eels − oils your wheels,
               I can't tell you how it feels
               When I see them jellied eels
               Jumping on the plate.

I like a jellied eel when it's misty (misty)
I like a jellied eel when it's hot
                    (She likes one when she's hot)
I like a jellied eel when I'm frisky (frisky)
I like a jellied eel when I'm not
                    (She likes one when she's not)

I'm always thinking of 'em
I simply 'ave to 'ave 'em,
When they're skipping down me throat
               I get a kind of spasm.

CHORUS

I like 'em when I'm sitting on me sofa (sofa)
I like 'em when I'm brooding in me bed
                    (She likes 'em in her bed)
I like 'em when I'm loafing with me loofa (loofa)
I like 'em when I'm standing on me head
                    (Standing on her head)

And when me money's spent
And I can't pay the rent
I cadge a jellied eel or two
               From some good natured gent.

CHORUS

(Spoken, very posh)
I like one when I'm chatting to the duchess (duchess)

I like one when I'm dining with the Duke
                          (She likes it with the Duke)
I like one when television I watches (watches)
I like one when I'm reading a good book
                          (She likes it with a book).

(sung)
Some folk like chicken fried
Or pies with meat inside
But jellied eels is all I need
                To keep me satisfied.

CHORUS

One of the most successful moments in the whole show was built round the 'Motorway Song', sung by Pat. Placed in front of him was a flower pot with a single daffodil. As Pat sang, Geoff came on with a big pair of shears and cut the flower down until only an inch of the stem remained. Bob produced a bucket and from the bucket Geoff poured cement mixture over the earth until the tiny stem disappeared; finally he levelled off the surface of the pot with a trowel. Simple, but very effective, and relating neatly to the Bus's ecological advert themes:

CHORUS: They're going to build a motorway through my back garden,
    No one can explain how I came to be chosen,
    They're going to build a motorway,
    They're ripping up the trees,
    Soon the lorries will be lurching through my cabbages and peas.

    Word came from the Council, it was all about a plan,
    Which I didn't understand,
    But it sounded very grand,
    They spoke of urban redevelopment,
    They said to ease the traffic flow
    A bit of my back yard would have to go.
    Well, I don't know,
    I suppose that those who've studied it must know best,
    And I wouldn't want my vegetable patch to hold up progress.

CHORUS: They're going to build a motorway, etc.

    My brother lives in Lilac Grove, it's just across the street,
    I've not seen him for weeks,
    We always used to meet
    And have a pint or two at the Old Dun Cow,
    It's just a heap of rubble now,
    The pawn shop's disappeared and so's
    The barber's where we always used to go.
    And I don't know,
    These noisy great machines are working non-stop,
    And funny things are growing and it looks as though the bomb's dropped.

CHORUS: The bulldozers are closing in on my back garden,
    No one can explain how I came to be chosen,

The bulldozers are closing in,
They've ripped up all the trees,
Soon the lorries will be zooming through my cabbages and peas.

I don't go out much any more, can't find my way around,
The wind nearly knocks me down,
There's tunnels underground
And just to get about from place to place
Is like a bleeding steeplechase,
Day and night the traffic flows,
It's best to plug your ears and hold your nose,
But I suppose,
I'm better off than some, don't think I'm just sour
And I'm grateful for the grandstand view I'm getting of the rush hour.

CHORUS: They've built an eight-lane motorway through my back garden,
No one can explain how I came to be chosen,
They've built an eight-lane motorway
They've ripped up all the trees,
Now lorries zoom where once I grew my cabbages and peas.

THE OTHER COMPANY

TOC — Henry Goodman, Judy Hepburn, Bill Patterson, Ken Shaw and Jill
Spurrier — maintained its identity as a formal theatre group on the Bus, while
developing a flexibility in keeping with the special conditions of fun and art.
Within a few weeks the players were varying their strictly scripted programmes
with spontaneous participatory work, especially when there were a lot of
children in the audience. One of the major impulses behind this pliability was
the presence of Henry Goodman, who came to Inter-Action with a wide
experience in variety entertainment. The result was a company that, while
holding the line of its performances, demonstrated increasingly extroverted
responses to its audience. TOC put on two shows: *The Bus Hijack Mystery* by
Neil Hornick, and an entertainment known inside Inter-Action as 'The Thespian
Show' — a composite of pieces, several of them taken from the Bus Repertoire,
and hinging on Jim Hiley's *Never Cross A Conductor.*

THE BUS HIJACK MYSTERY — NEIL HORNICK

Having contributed one or two sketches, Neil, director of the Phantom Captain
Theatre Combine, suggested to Ed and Naftali that it might be possible to create
a whole show based on the theme of a bus being hijacked en route. The three of
them worked out the details in a taxi on the way to Buckingham Palace where
Ed was having his photograph taken as a prospective property developer. Neil
then went off and wrote it as a send-up with three distinct pitches: the Bus
itself, as a bus; television reportage; and stock theatrical characterization. The
live part of the entertainment was composed in five episodes, which then became
the subject of intervening video-broadcasts, giving the passengers a feed-back on
the events that were taking place around them. Thus, for example, they might
see pictures of a police car chasing the bus they were travelling in, or an inter-
view with the conductor they had just witnessed being bound, gagged and

10. *Passengers On The Upper Deck*

11. *The Other Company: L to R: Judy Hepburn, Ken Shaw, Henry Goodman,*
    Bill Patterson and Jill Spurrier

hauled off. In the event the closed circuit television could not be used. However Naftali and Neil had prepared for this contingency – even in the script the two elements, theatre and television, were self-contained. For reasons of space, only the live part of the show is given below.

Each character or part in Neil's play is a combination of a number of traditional stereotypes: Nigel Horniman, for example, played on the Bus by Henry Goodman, is by turns a medical man, a clown, a coward and a hero. Gabriella Falk fashioned the costumes of the hijackers themselves in the style in which strip cartoons depict futuristic events. The idiom, near that of the goon-show, constantly changes gear, and for this Naftali was the ideal director. His outstanding control of every line and his genius for creating original stylizations brought out the piece's overall consistency, despite the many vicissitudes of plot.

The Bus Hijack Mystery

by Neil Hornick

The scene is the top deck of a London Bus. Each episode is followed by a TV interlude relayed on video TV in full view of the passengers.

A recorded 'VOICE OVER' keeps passengers up to date with the plot.

At the end of each episode the actors 'freeze'. The pose is broken at the start of the next instalment, after the recorded announcement.

Characters: NIGEL HORNIMAN, a randy dentist
MRS WITHERS, a pregnant passenger
SOPHIA SEMPRINI, girl commando
ALONZO, her strong-arm man
INSPECTOR TIMBER, a fair cop
THE CONDUCTOR

Episode One

NIGEL HORNIMAN is already seated. Enter MRS WITHERS, flustered. The CONDUCTOR is attending to the genuine passengers.

WITHERS (to HORNIMAN): Excuse me, do you mind if I take this seat?

HORNIMAN: Where do you want to take it?

WITHERS (unsmiling): I have to sit down. You see, I'm going to have a baby at any moment. I'm on my way to the hospital. I would have driven there but my husband, who is a police officer, has taken the car to hunt down criminals.

HORNIMAN: Well, if your husband's a policeman I suppose you must be genuine. Here's my seat. And in case of an accident – I may be of some help. I'm a dentist.

WITHERS: Why, thank you. It's not often one meets with such courtesy these days. There's no respect any more for pregnant women, policemen, war heroes or dentists – all the symbols of a decent clean-living society. It makes me worry what kind of world my baby's going to be born into.

HORNIMAN: Well, it's too late to change your mind now. Tell me, have you ever thought of your child entering the dentistry profession?

WITHERS: I can't say it occurred to me, no. We were thinking of a career in heavy industry or the armed services.

HORNIMAN: Don't be too hasty. Look here, allow me to give you my card. (He produces a large girly playing-card by mistake and hastily replaces it by a business card.) Oops, sorry, wrong card. Ah, that's better. You know, dentistry is a lively open-air profession. You might even say it's something you can really get your teeth into. When your baby's grown up a bit – say, twenty years old – bring him along to my surgery and I'll see what I can do to straighten him out. Incidentally, I couldn't help noticing a nasty cavity in one of your front incisors. When you're on your feet again I'd be glad to fill up the hole for you. Otherwise you have a very fine set of strong gleaming teeth.

WITHERS (flattered): How nice of you to say so. So have you. I wouldn't like to be caught napping at the end of your fork. (They both laugh.) As a matter of fact I was also rather struck by your powerful-looking shoulder-blades. I admire the way they stick out stiffly from your back.

HORNIMAN: Are you sure they're not my arms?

WITHERS: Not unless your head's the wrong way round.

HORNIMAN (laughing a shade nervously): Well, one never knows these days, what with chemical additives and the rising cost of living.

WITHERS (excited): Tell me, when can we meet? Let's go to your surgery now.

HORNIMAN: Madam, a word of warning from one with medical training. Wait until you've had your baby. It will be easier all round.

(SOPHIA SEMPRINI, girl commando, appears abruptly through a trap-door. Her accomplice, ALONZO, appears at the rear. Both carry guns.)

SOPHIA: All right, everyone, stay exactly where you are.

ALONZO: Dat's it. Stay where you are.

HORNIMAN: Where else can we go.

SOPHIA: Alonzo, tie up the conductor and guard the rear. (While he does this she calls down to the driver.) O.K., driver, keep going. And follow the instructions we gave you or you know what'll happen to you. (ALONZO is having difficulties with the CONDUCTOR's gag.)

ALONZO: Boss, this is a lousy gag.

SOPHIA: That's nothing, wait till you see the rest of the show.

WITHERS: What is this all about. I have to get somewhere in a hurry.

SOPHIA: O.K., now just keep cool, everyone. This is a hijack.

HORNIMAN: What did she say?

SOPHIA: Hi-jack.

HORNIMAN (extending his hand): Hi, Freda, long time no see.

SOPHIA: No-sey is the word for you, citizen. Any more of that and you're for the high jump.

HORNIMAN: High jump. But this is a bus not an aeroplane.

SOPHIA (menacingly): Ever tried jumping from the top of a double-decker?

HORNIMAN: No, but I have tried getting off at the traffic-lights. It's very dangerous —

ALONZO: What's he talking about, boss? He said this was a bus.

SOPHIA: That's right. It is a bus.

ALONZO: But I thought we were hijacking a Jumbo Jet.

SOPHIA: That's next week, stupid. This is practice for the big time.

ALONZO: What's the big time?

SOPHIA: High Noon.

HORNIMAN: Hi Doris, long time no see.

ALONZO: Boss, shall I plug this mug?

SOPHIA: Not yet, Alonzo, he's small beer.

HORNIMAN: That's right — I'm a beer mug.

SOPHIA: O.K., you've had your fun but now face facts. This bus is now completely under our control. And you are all in our power. So you play ball with us and we'll play ball with you.

HORNIMAN: I'll play ball with you any day of the week. Shall we say, Thursday at ten? We could begin with high-balls at my place.

SOPHIA: High-balls?

HORNIMAN: Hi Zelda. Long time no see.

WITHERS (agitated): Look here, I demand to know why we're being kept prisoner. I'm about to have a baby and have to get to the hospital urgently. I demand to be let off immediately.

ALONZO: Let off! Watch out, boss. I think she's some kind of bomb. She looks as if she's going to explode at any minute.

WITHERS: A bomb! Oh, my God, have you planted a bomb in here?

ALONZO: How could we plant a bomb in here? It wouldn't get much sun and rain.

HORNIMAN: Not only that, it says 'No Smoking'.

SOPHIA: That's where you're all wrong. We *have* planted a bomb in here. And it's going to blow us all, *all* to kingdom come — (She gives a maniacal laugh.)

(The Actors freeze.)

VOICE OVER: Why has an innocent London Bus been hijacked? Why are the passengers being kept prisoner without food or drink and tortured by excruciatingly bad jokes? Will they all be blown to kingdom come or to a completely different destination? Stand by for the next thrilling instalment of 'The Bus Hijack Mystery'!

Episode Two

VOICE OVER: A London bus has been commandeered by a ruthless gang of hijackers, the conductor bound and gagged, and the passengers menaced by threats of bombing. Now read on.

SOPHIA: That's where you're all wrong. We *have* planted a bomb in here. And it's going to blow us all, *all* to kingdom come – (She gives a maniacal laugh.) – unless you all co-operate.

WITHERS: Oh, my God. Have pity on my poor unborn baby. I demand to be released. I demand to consult my lawyer. I demand protection from the police. I demand a decent living wage. I demand the removal of sex magazines from the bookstalls. I demand the restoration of hanging. I demand a fair trial. I demand a second chance. I demand a second helping. I demand a walking talking dolly from Father Christmas. I demand some attention. (She breaks down in hysterical sobbing.)

HORNIMAN (to audience): I know she's terrible, but it's a pretty demanding role. (To hijackers.) You swine, you'll never get away with this. You may have the upper hand now but remember – we're English.

ALONZO: We're English too.

HORNIMAN: Really? My God, it's good to bump into another Englishman in this God-forsaken place. Staying here for long? Care for a spot of golf – ?

(ALONZO and HORNIMAN check diary dates.)

SOPHIA: Enough of this babble. I hereby proclaim this bus the property of the People's Republic of Depravia!

(She performs an elaborate ritual salute whenever Depravia is mentioned, always echoed but bungled by ALONZO.)

WITHERS: Why can't you just let me off and I'll catch another bus? That won't do any harm. You're a woman. Can't you see I might have my baby at any moment.

SOPHIA: I'm afraid not, you male chauvinist dupe. You see, *every bus* on this route has been hijacked by our organization.

HORNIMAN: Christ Almighty!

SOPHIA: No, it's an entirely different outfit. This is a big operation.

HORNIMAN: Yes, nurse, I think I need some oxygen.

ALONZO: You'll need a stretcher by the time we've finished with you.

HORNIMAN: But this lady has the contractions – perhaps she would find a stretcher more useful. Stretcher! Contractions? No? Never mind . . .

ALONZO: Boss, I've had enough of this creep. Why don't you let me work him over?

SOPHIA: Not yet, Alonzo. He could be useful to us.

WITHERS: For God's sake, stop tormenting us. What are you up to?

SOPHIA: Our aim is to bring the entire bus service system to a standstill.

HORNIMAN: You're too late. It's already been done by London Transport.

WITHERS: Well, look here, I could go by a different route. If you just drop me off at the next corner I'll go to the hospital another way. I could take the 293 from . . . (She babbles on about another route.)

SOPHIA: That won't do you much good either. You see, every bus on every route in London has been simultaneously hijacked and is now under our control.

ALONZO: Yeah, you're in a jam, folks.

HORNIMAN: We're always in a jam on London buses.

WITHERS: Then – this is a coup?

SOPHIA: Exactly.

ALONZO: But, boss, you said this was a putsch.

SOPHIA: No, it's a coup. A putsch is a lesbian.

ALONZO: Dat's funny. I thought a coup was what the Scots get their milk from.

SOPHIA: Coup! Putsch! Schmutsch! What does it matter? This is a takeover on a massive scale. Every London bus has been requisitioned by the People's Republic of Depravia! (Ritual salute.)

WITHERS: But what do you plan to do with all these buses?

ALONZO: Dat's right. What *do* we plan to do with them?

SOPHIA: Our first glorious task is to drive the buses to our specially built underground depots in Snowdonia and paint them – yellow!

HORNIMAN: You fiends.

WITHERS: You would paint London buses yellow! This is monstrous.

SOPHIA (laughing insanely): Yes, we'll stop at nothing to achieve our ends.

ALONZO (puzzled): How can we stop at nothing? I thought we were stopping at Snowdonia.

SOPHIA: Don't mind Alonzo. He may be a bit dim but he's loyal, trustworthy and tough as old dog-biscuits.

HORNIMAN: But why do you want to paint them yellow?

WITHERS: Yes, I am curious – yellow?

SOPHIA: That is only the first step in the masterplan. Once painted yellow, the buses are driven straight back to London, there to fulfil the glorious purposes of our great leader and saviour, Count Otto Depravia. (Ritual salute.)

HORNIMAN: Who is this Count Depravia?

SOPHIA: Count Depravia is a wealthy but lonely genius whose life is devoted to turning everything that exists into something else. Alonzo and I, for instance, were once lowly Social Security clerks; until we fell under the beneficent spell of Depravia. He convinced us of the worthiness, nay, the spiritual necessity of his mission. and so – here we are – his willing minions – as soon, if you are sensible, you will be too.

71

HORNIMAN: So at this very moment we are speeding towards Snowdonia?

SOPHIA: Correct — in convoy with all the other buses.

WITHERS: Oh, my poor baby. He will be born in a bus.

SOPHIA: So much the better. The newborn child will automatically become the first natural citizen of the People's Republic of Depravia. (Ritual salute.) What an honour. What a blessing. I envy you, madame.

HORNIMAN: I'm sure something could be arranged if you're really keen . . . But what happens when the buses return to London?

SOPHIA: Ah, every route has its place in the masterplan of turning everything into something else. One route will be turned into mobile zoos displaying different kinds of captive human beings. Another will consist of travelling pleasure-gardens of vice, complete with naked girls and youths beckoning lonely passers-by to join them. Yet another will torture its passengers by endlessly relaying the soundtrack of 'The Sound of Music' — (She launches into 'Edelweiss, Edelweiss'.)

HORNIMAN: But this means the end of civilisation as we know it. What about this route?

SOPHIA: On this route not only will all the buses be yellow — so will the surrounding terrain. Every part of the route visible from the bus will be painted yellow — pavements, buildings, pillar boxes, trees. No one will be allowed into the area unless wearing yellow clothes. Think of it — everything yellow — a gigantic masterpiece of Depravian art.

HORNIMAN: So you'd turn everything yellow — yellow! The colour of banana, of match-boxes, of vomit, of cowardice, of the Yellow Peril incarnate. Why, this is a return to the worst days of Fu Manchu.

ALONZO: And dat ain't all. It's not just the buses we're taking over, but cars, trains, aeroplanes, factories, cinemas, everything —

HORNIMAN: I'll not let you get away with this, you swine —

(HORNIMAN hurls himself upon the hijackers, there is a scuffle and he is subdued. ALONZO fails to fell him with a karate chop to the neck. SOPHIA succeeds with a single finger-thrust. ALONZO is now eager to get at him.)

ALONZO: Let me finish him off, boss. Let me cut his ears off and stuff them up his arse. Let me stamp all over his fingers. Let me carve his initials on his soles and throw him over Hungerford Bridge. Let me try out all the new tortures I learned at the Adult Education Centre. Just say the word, boss —

WITHERS (screams): I think my baby's coming —

VOICE OVER: Will the villainous Alonzo get the go-ahead to destroy Nigel Horniman, the passengers' one hope of freedom? Will the pregnant Mrs Withers give birth on the bus? Will Count Depravia succeed in his evil designs? Will the police arrive in time? Stand by, if you can bear it, for the next sweaty instalment of the Bus Hijack Mystery.

Episode Three

VOICE OVER: Nigel Horniman, a plucky young dentist, is menaced by unscrupulous hijackers in his unsuccessful attempt to oppose them.

ALONZO: Let me tear his toenails out, boss. Let me chew his liver and cut his tie to shreds —

WITHERS (screams): I think my baby's coming —

SOPHIA: Hold it, everyone —

ALONZO: How can we hold it? It hasn't come out yet.

SOPHIA: Nobody move. The police are on our trail. And what's more they know we're not really English.

ALONZO: Does that mean we can speak in our own native accents now —

(SOPHIA and ALONZO 'revert' to foreign accents.)

SOPHIA: Yes . . . Now listen, we don't have much time. You two have caused us nothing but trouble from the moment we hijacked this bus. Why couldn't you behave yourselves nicely like the other passengers, who will make useful tools in the lower echelons of our organization. I ought to have you killed but you show spirit. So I'm going to give you a chance. I'll have you both horribly slaughtered unless —

HORNIMAN: Yes?

SOPHIA: Unless you join us, Alonzo and I.

HORNIMAN: But I'm not an ordained minister.

SOPHIA: Not in matrimony, you idiot. You must become active members of Count Depravia's People's Republic. (Ritual salute.) Or I'll have Alonzo cut you into so many pieces you'll have a great future as confetti.

HORNIMAN: Well then, you give me no choice. I consent to join your organization. But remember I'm an Englishman — what's the salary?

SOPHIA: No salary. You do it for the greater glory of Depravia. All you get is — expenses and cigarette money.

ALONZO: What use is money made of cigarettes?

SOPHIA: We must work faster. I must train you in the art of hijacking so that you can help us overpower the police and go on to even greater hijacking triumphs. Now then there are several possibilities. Do you have it in you to be a stick-up man?

HORNIMAN: It depends where I have to stick it up . . . Couldn't I just be a willing tool? Or even a script-writer? I'm sure I could write better lines than these.

WITHERS: Be glad you've got some lines at all. I've had nothing to say for ten minutes — *and* I'm supposed to be having a baby. (She turns on the agony.) Help, help, I think my baby's on its way —

ALONZO: I've got a pretty useless part too. Couldn't I try to rape you or something to keep up the interest?

SOPHIA: Quiet, both of you . . . (To MRS WITHERS.) On your feet, you. (SOPHIA launches into audition manner.) Now then I want to see you both trying our first entrance. O.K.? Hurry it along, darlings, and take it from the top . . .

(HORNIMAN and WITHERS impersonate the hijackers.)

HORNIMAN: All right, everyone, stay exactly where you are.

WITHERS: Dat's it. Stay where you are.

ALONZO: Where else can we go?

SOPHIA: Shut up, stupid. No, no, no. Poor. Unconvincing. Couldn't you try to project a bit more and look more frightening. Try switching roles.

WITHERS: All right, everyone, stay exactly where you are.

HORNIMAN: Dat's it. Stay where you are.

SOPHIA: Terrible, terrible. Look, don't call us, we'll call you.

HORNIMAN: No, wait a moment, there is a problem doing this convincingly without guns. If we could borrow yours for a few moments that might help us get into the roles.

SOPHIA: Very well, then, if you must. God, these amateurs! I suppose you'll want the conductor too. Alonzo, give him your gun and bring forward the conductor.

(ALONZO releases and ungags the CONDUCTOR. No sooner is the gag off then he is bound and gaggged again by MRS WITHERS in character as ALONZO.)

HORNIMAN: All right, everyone, stay exactly where you are.

WITHERS: Dat's right, stay exactly where you are.

ALONZO: Where else can we go?

HORNIMAN: Alonzo, tie up the conductor. (The CONDUCTOR is rebound and regagged.)

WITHERS: Boss, this is a lousy gag.

HORNIMAN: That's nothing, wait till you see the rest of the show . . . On second thoughts, I don't think I will see the rest of the show. Get back here, Mrs Withers . . . (To SOPHIA and ALONZO.) All right, you two may be clever but you've forgotten one thing. I'm English. Not only that. I'm an English dentist — and in my book that means resourceful, tough, shrewd, athletic, wildly handsome. And armed to the teeth. So stay exactly where you are.

WITHERS: Dat's right. Stay exactly where you are.

ALONZO: Where else can we go?

SOPHIA: I may have forgotten one thing — that you are an English dentist, resourceful, tough, shrewd, athletic, wildly handsome and armed to the teeth — but you've forgotten one thing too — that I am a loyal minion of Count Otto Depravia and hence — (Produces another gun.) — ready for every emergency. Aha!

ALONZO (producing a gun): Aha!

(All four are now confronting each other. They speak in perfect unison.)

ALL: All right, drop that gun or I shoot . . . Did you hear what I said . . . I'll count to three and then . . . One . . .Two . . .

(A POLICEMAN bursts into the scence.)

POLICEMAN: All right, all of you, stay exactly where you are.

VOICE OVER: Who is the mysterious uniformed stranger who has burst in on the scene? Have the hijackers themselves been hijacked? Will it all end in a bloodbath or a birdbath? Keep your ears to the ground for the next stirring episode of the Bus Hijack Mystery.

Episode Four

VOICE OVER: Two passengers have outwitted the hijackers of a London bus. They are all deadlocked in a fatal confrontation when a British policeman bursts in upon the scene.

POLICEMAN: All right, all of you — stay exactly where you are.

ALL (unison): Where else can we go?

POLICEMAN (striding into the centre of their mutually threatening circle): Allow me to introduce myself. Inspector Timber of the Yard. Timber? Yard? Get it?

HORNIMAN: Things are really deteriorating now.

POLICEMAN: I have just 'boarded' this bus on the suspicion that it is in illegal hands. Is there any truth in this?

ALL (unison): A brilliant hunch, Inspector, you're right. And I've got the hijackers covered right now . . . You lying swine, you're the hijackers . . . *I'm* the hijacker? Don't be ridiculous. I'm a passenger —

POLICEMAN (sternly): That's enough. So you all claim to be ordinary passengers . . . Well, I'm nobody's fool, there's something very peculiar going on here, and I intend to find out what it is. Throw down your hands and put up your weapons — I mean, throw down your weapons and put up your hands.

(The others comply.)

WITHERS (pleading dramatically): Inspector, I'm going to have a baby at any moment. Please rush me to the nearest hospital —

SOPHIA (she and ALONZO revert to their 'assumed' English accents): It's a trick, Inspector. She's the leader of Count Depravia's mob and she's concealing a bomb underneath her maternity smock.

ALONZO: Yeah, I seen it.

POLICEMAN (to ALONZO): Not so fast. How do I know what you may be concealing under your trousers?

SOPHIA: Don't worry, Inspector. My friend here has nothing to conceal.

HORNIMAN: Inspector, I can see you're nobody's fool — except perhaps your own. There's one sure way of finding out the truth. You see the conductor at the end of the bus there. You may have noticed that he is completely bound and gagged. Why not get him to identify the real hijackers?

SOPHIA: This is just another trick, Inspector, to pull the wool over your eyes.

POLICEMAN: Wool! If wool is involved in this case, then I'm the man to unravel it. Now then, is this the conductor you mentioned?

HORNIMAN: Right again, Inspector. I can see there's no catching you out.

(The INSPECTOR removes the CONDUCTOR's gag.)

POLICEMAN: All right, you, are you the conductor of this bus?

CONDUCTOR: Am I on telly?

POLICEMAN: I'm afraid I'm not at liberty to divulge that to you – it's classical information. Now I want you to cast your eye around all the passengers here and see if you can identify the criminals who banged and ground you – I mean bound and gagged you.

CONDUCTOR: That's a bit difficult. It all happened a long time ago.

POLICEMAN: Do as I say, man, or it will go hard with you.

CONDUCTOR: That'll be a nice change – it's been going soft on me for years . . . (The CONDUCTOR looks the genuine passengers up and down.) Hm, they all look pretty shifty to me . . . I think it was this one . . . or maybe this one . . . (Ends up looking at INSPECTOR.) I don't remember you paying your fare.

POLICEMAN: Never mind that. (Angrily.) Who are the demon hijackers terrorizing London?

CONDUCTOR: Frankly, sir, it could have been any one of them. They all look like a bunch of villains to me.

(The INSPECTOR replaces the gag and bundles the CONDUCTOR away.)

POLICEMAN: You're bloody useless. I'll handle this myself. (Turns to ALONZO.) Your face is strangely familiar.

ALONZO: Maybe that's because we met a few minutes ago.

POLICEMAN: I've got a shrewd suspicion we met before that. Haven't I seen you behind bars?

ALONZO: Ah, could be, Inspector. I used to work for the Social Security handing out money to the unemployed.

POLICEMAN: You wouldn't be unemployed at the moment, would you?

ALONZO: No, I'm acting in a travelling theatre company. Not much of a part but it's better than the back-end of a horse in a Blackpool panto.

POLICEMAN (exasperated): Let's have it straight, man. Do you have a record?

ALONZO: Well, yes, I admit it. Quite a few. I've got Mantovani, some old Bill Haleys and a Readers Digest Light Music Sampler. But I got them all on the up and up, honest, boss –

POLICEMAN: All right, you, shut up, I'm not finished with you yet. (To

MRS WITHERS.) How about you, fatty? Is it true you've got a bomb under your smock?

WITHERS (laughing coyly): My dear Inspector Timber, is it likely? I'm a poor pregnant passenger desperately trying to get to hospital to have my baby. And this gentleman, who is a dentist, is innocent too. Let us go. These are the real culprits.

SOPHIA: It's a lie.

HORNIMAN: It's the tooth, the whole tooth and nothing but the tooth.

SOPHIA: She is the right-hand man of Count Otto Depravia.

WITHERS: How can I be his right-hand man? I'm a woman.

SOPHIA: That only proves how dreadfully perverted he is. Inspector, do your duty.

POLICEMAN (masterfully): Right, I've heard enough. Not only have I stumbled across a criminal conspiracy of gigantic proportions — but I have advance information that one of you is in fact Count Otto Depravia himself. (All execute ritual salute.) I therefore arrest you all.

HORNIMAN: Good, I could do with a-rest.

VOICE OVER: Has Inspector Timber made a hideous blunder? Will the pregnant Mrs Withers be the victim of a miscarriage of justice? Which of the passengers is in fact Count Otto Depravia? Keep tuned in to the most exciting serial since 'Dick Barton — Special Agent'. You know it makes sense.

Episode Five

VOICE OVER: Will Count Depravia succeed in taking over the country? Is this the end of the free world and the beginning of anarchy? Is this the beginning of the end or the end of the beginning? Or is it the beginning of the beginning? Who knows? Who cares?

SOPHIA: Inspector, do your duty.

POLICEMAN: Right, I've had enough. I arrest you all!

(He tears off HORNIMAN's false moustach.)

What have you got to say to that?

HORNIMAN: All right, I'll come clean. (Runs a sponge over his face.) I am not Nigel Horniman, a clean-limbed young dentist, but nor am I a hijacker. I am in reality Lord Longford and I am on the lookout for smut of every description, the filthier the better. I received word that this bus was to be the scene of rude and disgusting revels so I decided to investigate, using the nom-de-plume of Horniman. Mrs Withers, forgive me if I insulted you by seeming to find you attractive — we anti-pornographers must sometimes enter the enemy camp. Actually, of course, I find you wholly repulsive.

POLICEMAN: Did you say 'Mrs Withers'? But I am Police-Constable Withers, masquerading as an Inspector to impress you all with my credentials. And if I am Constable Withers then you must be my wife, Prudence Withers,

'Police News Housewife of the Year' and mother of my as yet unborn child.

WITHERS: I would indeed be your wife, Withers, if I were not already in reality — Count Otto Depravia himself!

ALL: Count Depravia! (All give ritual salute.)

WITHERS: Yes. For years I have been preparing for this takeover under the perfect cover — marriage to a British policeman — thus gaining access to secret Scotland Yard information. (To SOPHIA and ALONZO.) You blundering fools. Lucky I decided to check up on you. You've all but ruined my plan to turn everything into something other than what it is. But I'm not finished yet. You see, I really *have* got a bomb under my maternity smock.

(She lifts up her smock to reveal a bomb embedded in the belly of a doll strapped to her belly. The bomb is a transformed cassette tape-recorder which relays a sombre voice going 'tick-tock tick-tock . . . '.)

And I only have to throw this switch to blow us all to Kingdom Come.

ALONZO: Not so fast, Depravia. I knew it was you all along. For I am not really Alonzo, a dim-witted thug, but Captain Frank Sheet, an undercover agent working for Interpol. I arrest you in the name of the Father, the Son and the Holy Ghost! (He brandishes a crucifix in Depravia's face. Depravia cowers away.)

HORNIMAN: Holy Mackeral!

ALONZO: As for you, 'Constable Withers', you can drop your unconvincing disguise, for you are neither Constable nor Inspector, although not unknown in Scotland Yard files — as Mavis Fang, male impersonator extraordinary and police-uniform fetishist.

POLICEMAN (unbuttons his raincoat to reveal sexy panties and bra, high boots. Removes hat to reveal ribbon in hair): Hullo Sailor!

WITHERS: You mean that while I was impersonating Constable Withers' wife, she was impersonating Constable Withers?

ALONZO: Correct.

WITHERS: Hm, I thought our sex life was a bit peculiar. So — I have been foiled all round. And yet — isn't this misadventure right in the spirit of my grand design of turning everything into something else? If only . . . Ah what satisfaction it would be if it turned out that Sophia here was not one of my loyal minions, after all, but somebody completely different. Then I would defuse this bomb, call off the whole operation and go to my fate — fulfilled.

SOPHIA: Never fear, Depravia, you've won after all. For I am not Sophia Semprini, girl commando, but — (Change of manner.) — Doris Leggitt, just an ordinary housewife. I've been trying to catch the eye of a talent scout for years so that I can appear on 'Opportunity Knocks' with my unique Green Shield Stamp-licking routine.

WITHERS: AH, what bliss! Now I can take my punishment like a man — or a woman, as the case may be.

POLICEMAN: And let's have a big hand for Doris here, a plucky young contestant bursting with talent. Doris, the clapometer shows you have the finest dose of clap in show business. Congratulations from all of us here on the show and remember:

(The whole Company launch into a song* and dance off.)

If you're riding on a bus, listening to the rain
Don't make a fuss if it turns into a train
Just remember this, and take it from me
Nothing is ever what it seems to be

You may be flying in the air in what you thought was a plane
You may have even paid your fare, but find you're swinging from a crane
Then just remember this, and take it from me
Nothing is ever what it seems to be.

You may be walking down the street, smiling at the sky
And then you find your feet have just kicked a passer-by
Please remember this, and take it from me,
Nothing is ever what it seems to be.

(END)

THE THESPIAN SHOW

Like *The Bus Hijack Mystery*, TOC's other show was ultra-theatrical. Jim Hiley's *Never Cross a Conductor* provided an umbrella theme – that of the murderous conductor – under which other pieces were accomodated. An end-of-the-pier type concert party board the Bus and, at first to the annoyance and then to the fury of the clippie, begin to assert themselves. The clippie, portrayed as a habitual deprivee of attention and recognition, assumes a succession of increasingly outlandish guises under the cover of which he murders both players, who are also over-dressed as ham-orators, and one or two planted passengers. Directed by Noel Grieg, *The Thespian Show* had the flexibility of *There's No Bussiness Like Show Bussiness,* with much the same sort of purchasing power through the diversity of its inputs. Once again there was no final script or arrangement of the material, just a working order acquired through rehearsals.

*Song by Bill Patterson

12. *Ed Berman, Henry Goodman and Inter-Action's 'Moonmen'*

4 : The First Season of the Fun Art Bus

For its first season the Bus ran as part of the Borough Festivals of London 1972. Between May 4th and July 22nd it was on the road for fifty-nine days, averaging four to five shows or round trips a day. It visited Lewisham, Greenwich, Camden, Harrow, Barking, Redbridge, Newham, Waltham Forest, Brent, Bexley, Havering, Islington, Hammersmith and Sutton, as well as Bath on a special excursion, playing along the streets, or operating special rides for school children and old age pensioners. The Bus has since been to Munich, though due to the Israeli massacre there were no performances, and has made a tour of Northern England.

London Transport sold the vehicle to Inter-Action for £250. By the time all the hardware had been installed and the Bus had been decorated, capital costs had risen to just over £3,000. Main and additional personnel costs (which include an allowance for the back-up staff working in the central organization of Inter-Action), running costs and production costs took this figure to £10,000 by the end of July. Three quarters of this sum was recovered from booking fees, a small grant from the Arts Council of Great Britain and television fees (the B.B.C. made two films of the Bus, one for 'Nationwide', and one for 'Review'); the deficit was eventually made up through the generosity of Rank Xerox, who financed the journey to Munich. Daily hire varies according to whereabouts, but in London it comes out at considerably less than the £490 per week projected for the original Mobile Base. For public bodies it is still a very inexpensive way of bringing constructive entertainment to a great number of people from right across the class spectrum. Inter-Action makes only one stipulation: that nobody getting on the Bus should have to pay.

The theatre deck has a capacity for thirty to forty passengers, according to size. The players found themselves performing to full houses upwards of eighty per cent of the season. The Kinetic Window Boxes attracted large crowds — one hundred and fifty, two hundred or more. Sometimes the Bus is run in conjunction with other Inter-Action activities. In Newham one afternoon, for example, the Bus stood still while the participatory street play, *Technicolour Peelers,* was performed by the Dogg's Troupe with two hundred and fifty people.

PURPOSES AND REACTIONS

The Fun Art Bus obviously reached its audiences. It provided entertainment where entertainment was least expected, and for people who are not accustomed to getting much away from the television set. Subsumed within these functions were other purposes, implicit in the kind of environmental theatre Ed had created. He wanted people to change their ideas about public transport, to see that travelling on a municipal bus does not necessarily have to be the grey and bleak experience it usually is. Perhaps anyone who has seen The Thespian Show will have more sympathy for bus conductors in future. Of course, there are those who did not enjoy themselves on the Bus, those who were not entertained. There would have been something wrong if it had appealed to the afficionados of avant-garde theatre. There have been very few of these, however: the joy of the Bus is that it is self-advertising, and so it is easier to select its audiences — or at least guarantee a diversity. Otherwise there was no simple category of disappointed passenger. One or two faces would remain determinedly glum, probably because of mood-factors beyond anyone's control. And just once in a while a prude might be upset, for example, by the transvestite capers in the *Hijack Mystery.* Even so, though they were free to leave they stayed. For the great majority of people persuaded to come out of their daily routines — and this rupture is one of the Bus's sub-purposes — there is no lack of reward. On nearly every trip a feeling of togetherness has been created on the top deck. Once in a while pensioners and school children are taken on board on the same trip, and it is always remarkable how well these two groups, normally so isolated from each other, interact on such occasions.

At one point it was put to Ed — wouldn't it be simpler to take the Dogg's Troupe or The Other Company on board an ordinary bus and let them perform to completely unsuspecting passengers? Why bother about a special Fun Art Bus?

The difficulty with guerilla theatre, which is what this suggested alternative amounts to, is that too much of its energy has to be dissipated in overcoming or bringing round the audience which, quite legitimately, is likely to feel that it is being targetted. There is also a tendency to over-boost the egos of the actors. Ed never wanted the Bus to shock people; rather he wanted it to be a means of treating with people. Passengers on the Fun Art Bus are an audience by virtue of their own will, and not of anybody else's. It is essential that this should be so if any kind of participation, involvement or productive interaction between the audience and the players is to be achieved. Thus, it quite often happened in the first season that, when the Bus was making several trips from

81

the same stop, one or two people were reluctant to climb on board when the Bus first appeared, but joined up later, on the second or third trip.

There was one operational failure: the Bus did not work on a stop-by-stop basis, as Ed had intended it should, passengers getting on and off, using the Bus as a means of transport on actual routes. There were several reasons for this. Passengers might have been apprehensive as to whether the Bus really was following the stated route; it would have been more difficult to sustain the entertainment on the theatre deck; but most of all, once people were on board, they wanted to stay. The round trip, lasting anything from less than thirty minutes to the full hour, was the most satisfactory arrangement from every point of view.

As an event that convincingly disrupts the traditional equation between achievement and seriousness, the Bus stresses the importance of voluntary participation. Audience participation exists in several forms. There is participation through physical placement — environmental participation: this the Bus provides in full measure. There is participation through 'joining in' the entertainment — singing songs, keeping up one end of a dialogue, or, more simply, organized clapping. The Bus provides ideal circumstances for this as well. Sometimes the theatre deck has been used as a participatory drama space. For example, in the first season two members of TOC — Ken and Judy perhaps — would improvise an easy situation, tough guy meets dolly bird.

At crucial moments of interchange, the audience would be asked to supply a line of dialogue. After this a volunteer would be called to take over Ken's part; and then a reverse situation in which a girl would substitute for Judy, the audience now giving actional directions as well as dialogue. Within a very short time, and with very little assistance from the actors, the audience of school children were constructing a whole drama by themselves.

The key to audience participation is actor participation. On the Fun Art Bus there is very little between the players and the passengers, the joke proscenium arch apart. And, because the players perform as much as possible up and down the aisle and in the seats, the audience becomes involved in a shared relationship with their surroundings. As the Bus moves along the actors struggle to maintain their balance, and the audience sways with them. This process maximizes the amount of energy released; and this energy can be channeled into a further extension of the relationships that have already come into being, and, if it is desired, even into putting across certain items of information and knowledge. Ed has a 'thing' about movement and rhythm in relation to creativity: 'motion begets emotion and rhythm begets harmonies'; whatever it means it happened on the Bus.

It is hoped that, besides being entertained on the Bus, some people will be sufficiently aroused to want to inquire further of the troupes they have seen, and of Inter-Action itself. There are in fact any number of possible spin-offs. Who knows? — even London Transport might do something to brighten itself up — print poetry on their tickets, although it will be a long time before they give them away free. As more than one passenger was overheard to ask when they got off the magic transport — 'Why can't all buses be Fun Art Buses?'.

Afterword by Ed Berman

There is a joke in Inter-Action: 'If it succeeds, call it "success". If it fails, call it a "pilot project".' The Fun Art Bus is both a genuine pilot project and a success.

We did not get people to use the Bus as a means of public transport. They would not get off at a point along the way. Rather they seemed to want to come back to where they started. Hopefully there is no allegory involved in this.

Any environment is a theatre. The more traffic (foot or motor) the better. Marble Arch is the best outdoor theatre in England. It is also the most expensive theatre set ever built. It is also an obstruction to traffic that wants to go in a straight line from Park Lane to the Edgware Road without passing GO. It depends on how you look at it. When we performed James Saunders' *Dog Accident!* at Marble Arch, we used the fact that it is cut off by traffic to isolate our audience and lend credence to the fact that a dog could have been killed by the whirring cars.

Since Inter-Action was established in 1968 we have explored the potential of fixed and mobile environments for theatrical purposes. We have done this because our purposes are mainly social. Ultimately our use of the theatre is a focusing instrument for social issues and, even more important, social processes.

Can theatre integrate into our daily lives again. Only if it integrates into our daily environment. Either theatres remain special boxes for special occasions for special people or they become useful spaces for useable purposes for usual people. Or we treat everyday spaces in an uncommon way bringing new meanings and relationships out of old alphabets.

The Fun Art Bus had to develop a total visual and dramatic language if it were to become more than simply a gimmicky bottle for the old wine.

This attention to the necessity of matching content wtih new forms provides an excitement and potential beyond the limits of ordinary theatre. It challenges creators to implement their ideas, to make them work with people to whom they may be relevant. Brecht at the Royal Court is the emperor with clothes on. Even the magic has gone and everybody has seen it all before.

The Fun Art Bus is an attempt at magic — changing a total environment and moving it to where it might be meaningful as an accidental confrontation. And this with people who never expected to be challenged at all.

Appendix

Music to the Songs by Leon Rosselson

The Fun Art Bus is the bus of the people

Leon Rosselson

The Fun Art Bus is the bus of the peo-ple, step on board the Fun Art Bus, No need to rush, Don't have to fuss, If you come with us on the Fun Art Bus, Step on board the bus of the peo-ple Step on board the Fun Art Bus. Of all the in-ventions the world has e-ver seen, like the tel-e-phone, the mo-tor car and mar-gar-ine, There's none can com-pare with this mag-ic-al machine, This mag-ic-al machine, The Fun Art Bus.

Bus Busker's Song

Leon Rosselson

We've come to en-ter-tain you, We've come to en-ter-tain you, We've come to en-ter-tain you, It's busking time, We're the time. We've played all the buses from Hamp-stead to Kew, From the twelve A to Croy-don and the se-ven-ty two And the se-ven-ty four to Earl's Court and the zoo, We're the bus-kers, the bus-kers, the bus-kers. We're buskers —

R.G. Barr, Superstar

Leon Rosselson

Hoo-ter's gone Clock-ing on Ev'-ry Mon-day mor-ning. On the job Turn-ing knobs Just a ma-chine. But watch me on a Sat-ur-day That's when I make my get-a-way R. G. Barr is on dis-play Do-ing his thing R. G. Barr Su-per-star Wi-zard on the old guitar R. G. Barr A Hear 'em scream I'm their dream R. G. Barr is King ——

The Tallest Man in the World

Leon Rosselson

When I was just a lit-tle ti-ny tot, My fa-ther al-ways used to say to me, Walk tall my son and you'll be ten-foot high, In-stead of be-ing on-ly two foot three. And so I de-cid-ed to grow, Because I knew that if I grew I would be some-one some-one They would look up to me be-cause I was some-one

They would ad-mire me be-cause I was some-one, They couldn't ig-nore me, They would say when they saw me (SPOKEN) Look at him - he's someone Be-cause ev'-ry-one loves some-one, Be-cause ev'-ry-one loves some-one.

Jellied Eels

Leon Rosselson

CHORUS

Jel-lied eels Jel-lied eels, Jump-ing on the plate. Jel-lied eels Jel-lied eels I can hard-ly wait, Jel-lied eels oils your wheels I can't tell you how it feels When I see them Jel-lied eels — jump-ing on the plate

VERSE

I like a jel-lied eel when it's mis-ty (mis-ty) I like a jel-lied eel when it's hot (she likes one when she's hot) I like a jel-lied eel when I'm fris-ky (fris-ky) I like a jel-lied eel when I'm not (she likes one when she's not) I'm al-ways think-ing of 'em, I simply 'ave to 'ave 'em. When they're slipping down my throat I get a kind of spas-m ———

They're going to build a motorway through my back garden

Leon Rosselson

CHORUS Em ... Am ... B7

They're going to build a mo-tor-way through my back gar-den, No-one can explain how

Em

I came to be cho-sen, They're going to build a mo-tor-way, They're

Am ... B7

rip-ping up the trees, Soon the lorries will be lurch-ing through my

Em F# ... VERSE Am ... C

cab-bag-es and peas. Word came from the coun-cil it was

E ... B7

all a-bout a plan, which I didn't un-der-stand But it

E ... A

sound-ed ve-ry grand, They spoke of ur-ban re-de-vel-op-ment, And im-

E ... F#

prov-ing the en-vir-on-ment, They said to ease the traf-fic flow, A

B ... B7

bit of my back-yard would have to go. Well I don't know, I sup-

E#

pose that those who've studied it must know best, And I would-n't want my

B ... B7

veg-et-ab-le patch to hold up pro-gress, They're

METHUEN PLAYSCRIPTS

Paul Ableman	TESTS
	BLUE COMEDY
Andrei Amalrik	EAST-WEST and IS UNCLE JACK A CONFORMIST?
Barry Bermange	NATHAN AND TABILETH and OLDENBERG
John Bowen	THE CORSICAN BROTHERS
Howard Brenton	REVENGE
	CHRISTIE IN LOVE AND OTHER PLAYS
	PLAYS FOR PUBLIC PLACES
Henry Chapman	YOU WON'T ALWAYS BE ON TOP
Peter Cheeseman (Ed)	THE KNOTTY
Caryl Churchill	OWNERS
David Cregan	THREE MEN FOR COLVERTON
	TRANSCENDING and THE DANCERS
	THE HOUSES BY THE GREEN
	MINIATURES
Rosalyn Drexler	THE INVESTIGATION and HOT BUTTERED ROLL
Simon Gray	THE IDIOT
Henry Livings	GOOD GRIEF!
	THE LITTLE MRS FOSTER SHOW
	HONOUR AND OFFER
	PONGO PLAYS 1–6
	THIS JOCKEY DRIVES LATE NIGHTS
	THE FFINEST FFAMILY IN THE LAND
John McGrath	EVENTS WHILE GUARDING THE BOFORS GUN
David Mercer	THE GOVERNOR'S LADY
Georges Michel	THE SUNDAY WALK
Rodney Milgate	A REFINED LOOK AT EXISTENCE
Guillaume Oyono-Mbia	THREE SUITORS: ONE HUSBAND and UNTIL FURTHER NOTICE
Alan Plater	CLOSE THE COALHOUSE DOOR
David Selbourne	THE PLAY OF WILLIAM COOPER AND EDMUND DEW-NEVETT
	THE TWO-BACKED BEAST
	DORABELLA
Wole Soyinka	CAMWOOD ON THE LEAVES
Johnny Speight	IF THERE WEREN'T ANY BLACKS YOU'D HAVE TO INVENT THEM
Martin Sperr	TALES FROM LANDSHUT
Boris Vian	THE KNACKER'S ABC
Lanford Wilson	HOME FREE! and THE MADNESS OF LADY BRIGHT

Harrison, Melfi, Howard	NEW SHORT PLAYS: 1
Duffy, Harrison, Owens	NEW SHORT PLAYS: 2
Barker, Grillo, Haworth, Simmons	NEW SHORT PLAYS: 3

METHUEN'S MODERN PLAYS

Edited by John Cullen and Geoffrey Strachan

Paul Ableman	GREEN JULIA
Jean Anouilh	ANTIGONE
	BECKET
	POOR BITOS
	RING ROUND THE MOON
	THE LARK
	THE REHEARSAL
	THE FIGHTING COCK
	DEAR ANTOINE
John Arden	SERJEANT MUSGRAVE'S DANCE
	THE WORKHOUSE DONKEY
	ARMSTRONG'S LAST GOODNIGHT
	LEFT-HANDED LIBERTY
	SOLDIER, SOLDIER AND OTHER PLAYS
	TWO AUTOBIOGRAPHICAL PLAYS
John Arden and Margaretta d'Arcy	THE BUSINESS OF GOOD GOVERNMENT
	THE ROYAL PARDON
	THE HERO RISES UP
Ayckbourn, Bowen, Brook, Campton, Melly, Owen, Pinter, Saunders, Weldon	MIXED DOUBLES
Brendan Behan	THE QUARE FELLOW
	THE HOSTAGE
Barry Bermange	NO QUARTER and THE INTERVIEW
Edward Bond	SAVED
	NARROW ROAD TO THE DEEP NORTH
	THE POPE'S WEDDING
	LEAR
John Bowen	LITTLE BOXES
	THE DISORDERLY WOMEN
Bertolt Brecht	MOTHER COURAGE
	THE CAUCASIAN CHALK CIRCLE
	THE GOOD PERSON OF SZECHWAN
	THE LIFE OF GALILEO

Syd Cheatle	STRAIGHT UP
Shelagh Delaney	A TASTE OF HONEY
	THE LION IN LOVE
Max Frisch	THE FIRE RAISERS
	ANDORRA
Jean Giraudoux	TIGER AT THE GATES
Simon Gray	SPOILED
	BUTLEY
Peter Handke	OFFENDING THE AUDIENCE and
	SELF-ACCUSATION
	KASPAR
Rolf Hochhuth	THE REPRESENTATIVE
Heinar Kipphardt	IN THE MATTER OF J. ROBERT
	OPPENHEIMER
Arthur Kopit	CHAMBER MUSIC AND OTHER PLAYS
	INDIANS
Jakov Lind	THE SILVER FOXES ARE DEAD AND
	OTHER PLAYS
David Mercer	ON THE EVE OF PUBLICATION
	AFTER HAGGERTY
	FLINT
John Mortimer	THE JUDGE
	FIVE PLAYS
	COME AS YOU ARE
	A VOYAGE ROUND MY FATHER
Joe Orton	CRIMES OF PASSION
	LOOT
	WHAT THE BUTLER SAW
	FUNERAL GAMES and THE GOOD AND
	FAITHFUL SERVANT
Harold Pinter	THE BIRTHDAY PARTY
	THE ROOM and THE DUMB WAITER
	THE CARETAKER
	A SLIGHT ACHE AND OTHER PLAYS
	THE COLLECTION and THE LOVER
	THE HOMECOMING
	TEA PARTY AND OTHER PLAYS
	LANDSCAPE and SILENCE
	OLD TIMES
David Selbourne	THE DAMNED
Jean-Paul Sartre	CRIME PASSIONNEL
Wole Soyinka	MADMEN AND SPECIALISTS
	THE JERO PLAYS
Boris Vian	THE EMPIRE BUILDERS
Peter Weiss	TROTSKY IN EXILE
Theatre Workshop and	
Charles Chilton	OH WHAT A LOVELY WAR

Charles Wood   'H'
                      VETERANS
Carl Zuckmayer   THE CAPTAIN OF KOPENICK

If you would like further information
about Methuen plays, please write to
The Marketing Department
Eyre Methuen Ltd
11 New Fetter Lane
London EC4P 4EE